Puffin Classics

WHAT KATY DID NEXT

Three years after returning home from Hillsover board-ing school to the small American town of Burnet, Katy Carr receives an unexpected and thrilling invitation – to go to Europe for a year with Mrs Ashe and her young daughter, Amy. Although the prospect of being separated from her beloved family is unsettling, the lure of magnificent, romantic cities is too much for Katy, and she is soon setting off on what turns out to be an unforgettable adventure in more ways than one!

Born in Cleveland, Ohio, in 1835, Susan Coolidge wrote three hugely successful books about Katy Carr: *What Katy Did* (1872), *What Katy Did at School* (1873) and *What Katy Did Next* (1886). All three are published in Puffin Classics, complete and unabridged.

Susan Coolidge

WHAT KATY
DID NEXT

PUFFIN BOOKS

Puffin Books, Penguin Books Ltd, Harmondsworth, Middlesex, England
Viking Penguin Inc., 40 West 23rd Street, New York, New York 10010, USA
Penguin Books Australia Ltd, Ringwood, Victoria, Australia
Penguin Books Canada Ltd, 2801 John Street, Markham, Ontario, Canada L3R 1B4
Penguin Books (NZ) Ltd, 182–190 Wairau Road, Auckland 10, New Zealand

First published 1886
Published in Puffin Books 1986

Made and printed in Great Britain by
Cox and Wyman Ltd, Reading
Typeset in Linotron Palatino
by Rowland Phototypesetting Ltd,
Bury St Edmunds, Suffolk

CONTENTS

CHAPTER

1

AN UNEXPECTED GUEST

The September sun was glinting cheerfully into a pretty
bedroom furnished with blue. It danced on the glossy
hair and bright eyes of two girls, who sat together hem-
ming ruffles for a white muslin dress. The half-finished
skirt of the dress lay on the bed, and as each crisp ruffle
was completed, the girls added it to the snowy heap,
which looked like a drift of transparent clouds or a pile
of foamy white of egg beaten stiff enough to stand
alone.

These girls were Clover and Elsie Carr, and it was
Clover's first evening dress for which they were hem-
ming ruffles. It was nearly two years since a certain visit
made by Johnnie to Inches Mills, of which some of you
have read in *Nine Little Goslings*, and more than three
since Clover and Katy had returned home from the
boarding school at Hillsover.

Clover was now eighteen. She was a very small Clover
still, but it would have been hard to find anywhere a
prettier little maiden than she had grown to be. Her skin
was so exquisitely fair that her arms and wrists and
shoulders, which were round and dimpled like a baby's,

seemed cut out of daisies or white rose leaves. Her thick, brown hair waved and coiled gracefully about her head. Her smile was peculiarly sweet, and the eyes, always Clover's chief beauty, had still that pathetic look which made them quite irresistible to anyone with a tender or sympathetic heart.

Elsie, who adored Clover, considered her as beautiful as girls in books, and was proud to be permitted to hem ruffles for the dress in which she was to burst upon the world. Though, as for that, not much 'bursting' was possible in Burnet, where tea parties of a middle-aged description, and now and then a mild little dance, represented 'gaiety' and 'society'. Girls 'came out' very much as the sun comes out in the morning – by slow degrees and gradual approaches, with no particular one moment which could be fixed upon as having been the crisis of the joyful event.

'There,' said Elsie, adding another ruffle to the pile on the bed, 'there's the fifth done. It's going to be ever so pretty, I think. I'm glad you had it all white; it's a great deal nicer.'

'Cecy wanted me to have a blue bodice and sash,' said Clover, 'but I wouldn't. Then she tried to persuade me to get a long spray of pink roses for the skirt.'

'I'm so glad you didn't! Cecy was always crazy about pink roses. I only wonder she didn't wear them when she was married!'

Yes, the excellent Cecy, who at thirteen had announced her intention to devote her whole life to teaching Sunday School, visiting the poor, and setting a good example to her more worldly contemporaries, had actually forgotten these fine resolutions, and before she was twenty had become the wife of Sylvester Slack, a young lawyer in a neighbouring town! Cecy's wedding and wedding clothes, and Cecy's house furnishing, had been the great excitement of the preceding year in Burnet; and a fresh excitement had come since in the shape of Cecy's baby, now about two months old, and named 'Katherine Clover', after her two friends. This made it natural that Cecy and her affairs should still be of interest in the Carr household, and Johnnie, at the time we write of, was making her a week's visit.

'She *was* rather wedded to them,' went on Clover, pursuing the subject of the pink roses. 'She was almost vexed when I wouldn't buy the spray. But it cost lots, and I didn't want it in the least, so I stood firm. Besides, I always said that my first party dress should be plain white. Girls in novels always wear white to their first balls and fresh flowers are a great deal prettier, anyway, than artificial. Katy says she'll give me some violets to wear.'

'Oh, will she? That will be lovely!' cried the adoring Elsie. 'Violets look just like you, somehow. Oh, Clover, what sort of a dress do you think I shall have when I grow up and go to parties and things? Won't it be awfully interesting when you and I go out to choose it?'

Just then the noise of someone running upstairs quickly made the sisters look up from their work. Footsteps are very significant at times, and these footsteps suggested haste and excitement.

Another moment and the door opened, and Katy dashed in calling out, 'Papa – Elsie, Clover, where's papa?'

'He went over the river to see that son of Mr White's who broke his leg. Why, what's the matter?' asked Clover.

'Is somebody hurt?' inquired Elsie, startled at Katy's agitated looks.

'No, not hurt; but poor Mrs Ashe is in such trouble!'

Mrs Ashe, it should be explained, was a widow who had come to Burnet some months previously, and had taken a pleasant house not far from the Carrs'. She was a pretty, ladylike woman, with a particularly graceful, appealing manner, and very fond of her one child, a little girl. Katy and Papa both took a fancy to her at once, and the families had grown neighbourly and intimate in a short time, as people occasionally do when circumstances are favourable.

'I'll tell you all about it in a minute,' went on Katy. 'But first I must find Alexander, and send him off to meet Papa and beg him to hurry home.' She went to the head of the stairs as she spoke, and called 'Debby! Debby!' Debby answered. Katy gave her direction, and then came back again to the room where the other two were sitting.

'Now,' she said, speaking more collectedly, 'I must explain as fast as I can, for I have got to go back. You know that Mrs Ashe's little nephew is here for a visit, don't you?'

'Yes, he came on Saturday.'

'Well, he was ailing all day yesterday, and today he is worse, and she is afraid it is scarlet fever. Luckily, Amy was spending the day with the Uphams yesterday, so she scarcely saw the boy at all; and as soon as her mother became alarmed, she sent Amy out into the garden to play, and hasn't let her come indoors since, so she can't have been exposed to any particular danger yet. I went by the house on my way down street, and there sat the poor little thing all alone in the arbour, with her dolly in her lap, looking so disconsolate. I spoke to her over the fence, and Mrs Ashe heard my voice, and opened the upstairs window and called to me. She said Amy had never had the fever, and that the very idea of her having it frightened her to death. She is such a delicate child, you know.'

'Oh, poor Mrs Ashe!' cried Clover, 'I am so sorry for her! Well, Katy, what did you do?'

'I hope I didn't do wrong, but I offered to bring Amy here. Papa won't object, I am almost sure.'

'Why, of course he won't. Well?'

'I am going back now to fetch Amy. Mrs Ashe is to let Ellen, who hasn't been in the room with the little boy, pack a bagful of clothes and put it out on the steps, and I shall send Alexander for it by and by. You can't think how troubled poor Mrs Ashe was. She couldn't help crying when she said that Amy was all she had left in the world. And I nearly cried too, I was so sorry for her. She was so relieved when I said that we would take Amy. You know she has a great deal of confidence in Papa.'

'Yes, and in you, too. Where will you put Amy to sleep, Katy?'

'What do you think would be best? In Dorry's room?'

'I think she'd better come in here with you, and I'll go into Dorry's room. She is used to sleeping with her mother, you know, and she would be lonely if she were left to herself.'

'Perhaps that will be better, only it is a great bother for you, Clovy dear.'

'I don't mind,' responded Clover cheerfully. 'I rather like to change about and try a new room once in a while. It's as good as going on a journey – almost.'

She pushed aside the half-finished dress as she spoke, opened a drawer, took out its contents, and began to carry them across the entrance to Dorry's room, doing everything with the orderly deliberation that was characteristic of whatever Clover did. Her preparations were almost complete before Katy returned, bringing with her little Amy Ashe.

Amy was a tall child of eight, with a frank, happy face, and long light hair hanging down her back. She looked like the pictures of *Alice in Wonderland*, but just at that moment it was a very woeful little Alice indeed that she resembled, for her cheeks were stained with tears and her eyes swollen with recent crying.

'Why, what is the matter?' cried kind little Clover, taking Amy in her arms, and giving her a great hug. 'Aren't you glad that you are coming to make us a visit? We are.'

'Mamma didn't kiss me for goodbye,' sobbed the little girl. 'She didn't come downstairs at all. She just put her head out of the window and said, "Goodbye, Amy! be very good, and don't make Miss Carr any trouble," and then she went away. I never went anywhere before without kissing mamma goodbye.'

'Mamma was afraid to kiss you for fear she might give you the fever,' explained Katy, taking her turn as a comforter. 'It wasn't because she forgot. She felt worse about it than you did, I imagine. You know the thing she cares most for is that you shall not be ill as your cousin Walter is. She would rather do anything than have that happen. As soon as he gets well she will kiss you dozens of times, see if she doesn't. Meanwhile, she says in this note that you must write her a little letter every day, and she will hang a basket by a string out of the window, and you and I will go and drop the letters into the basket, and stand by the gate and see her pull it up. That will be funny, won't it? We will play that you are my little girl, and that you have a real mamma and a make-believe mamma.'

'Shall I sleep with you?' demanded Amy.

'Yes, in that bed over there.'

'It's a pretty bed,' pronounced Amy after examining it gravely for a moment. 'Will you tell me a story every morning?'

'If you don't wake me up too early. My stories are always sleepy till seven o'clock. Let us see what Ellen has packed in that bag, and then I'll give you some drawers of your own, and we will put the things away.'

The bag was full of neat little frocks and underclothes stuffed hastily in together. Katy took them out, smoothing the folds, and crimping the tumbled ruffles with her fingers. As she lifted the last skirt, Amy, with a cry of joy, pounced on something that lay beneath it.

'It is Maria Matilda,' she said; 'I'm glad of that. I thought Ellen would forget her, and the poor child wouldn't know what to do, with me and her little sister not coming to see her for so long. She was having the measles on the back shelf of the closet, you know, and nobody would have heard her if she had cried ever so loud.'

'What a pretty face she has!' said Katy, taking the doll out of Amy's hands.

'Yes, but not so pretty as Mabel. Miss Upham says that Mabel is the prettiest child she ever saw. Look, Miss Clover,' lifting the other doll from the table where she had laid it, 'hasn't she got *sweet* eyes? She's older than Maria Matilda, and she knows a great deal more. She's begun on French verbs!'

'Not really! Which ones?'

'Oh! Only "*j'aime, tu aimes, il aime*", you know – the

same that our class is learning at school. She hasn't tried any but that. Sometimes she says it quite nicely, but sometimes she's very stupid, and I have to scold her.' Amy had quite recovered her spirits by this time.

'Are these the only dolls you have?'

'Oh, please don't call them that!' urged Amy. 'It hurts their feelings dreadfully. I never let them know that they are dolls. They think that they are real children, only sometimes, when they are very bad, I use the word for a punishment. I've got several other children. There's old Ragazza. My uncle named her, and she's made of rag, but she has such bad rheumatism that I don't play with her any longer; I just give her medicine. Then there's Effie Deans – she's only got one leg; and Mopsa the Fairy – she's a tiny one made out of china; and Peg of Linkinvaddy – but she don't count, for she's come all to pieces.'

'What very queer names your children have!' said Elsie, who had come in during the enumeration.

'Yes; Uncle Ned named them. He's a very funny uncle, but he's nice. He's always so much interested in my children.'

'There's papa now!' cried Katy, and she ran downstairs to meet him.

'Did I do right?' she asked anxiously, after she had told her story.

'Yes, my dear, perfectly right,' replied Dr Carr. 'I only hope Amy was taken away in time. I will go round at once to see Mrs Ashe and the boy; and, Katy, keep away from me when I come back, and keep the others away, till I have changed my coat.'

It is odd how soon and how easily human beings accustom themselves to a new condition of things. When sudden illness comes, or sudden sorrow, or a house is burned up, or blown down by a tornado, there are a few hours or days of confusion and bewilderment, and then people gather up their wits and their courage and set to work to repair damage. They clear away ruins, plant and rebuild, very much as ants whose hill has been trodden upon, and who, after running wildly about for a little while, begin all together to reconstruct the cone of sand which is so important in their eyes. In a very short time the changes which at first seem so sad and strange become accustomed and matter-of-course things which no longer surprise us.

It seemed to the Carrs after a few days as if they had always had Amy in the house with them. Papa's daily visit to the sick room, their avoidance of him till after he had 'changed his coat', Amy's lessons and games of play, her dressing and undressing, the walks with the make-believe mamma, the dropping of notes into the little basket, seemed part of a system of things which had been going on for a long, long time, and which everybody would miss should they suddenly stop.

But they by no means suddenly stopped. Little Walter Ashe's case proved to be rather a severe one, and after he had begun to mend, he caught cold somehow and was taken worse again. There were some serious symptoms, and for a few days Dr Carr did not feel sure how things would turn. He did not speak of his anxiety at home, but kept silence and a cheerful face, as doctors know how to do. Only Katy, who was more intimate with her father than the rest, guessed that things were going gravely at the other house, and she was too well trained to ask questions. The threatening symptoms passed off, however, and little Walter slowly got better; but it was a long convalescence, and Mrs Ashe grew thin and pale before he began to look rosy. There was no one on whom she could devolve the charge of the child. His mother was dead; his father, an over-worked business man, had barely time to come once a week to see about him, and there was no one at his home but a housekeeper, in whom Mrs Ashe had not full confidence. So the good aunt denied herself the sight of her own child, and devoted her strength and time to Walter; nearly two months passed, and still little Amy remained at Dr Carr's.

She was entirely happy there. She had grown very fond of Katy, and was perfectly at home with the others. Phil, and Johnnie, who had returned from her visit to Cecy, were by no means too old or too proud to be playfellows to a child of eight; and with all the older members of the family Amy was a chosen pet. Debby baked turnovers, and twisted cinnamon cakes into all sorts of fantastic shapes to please her; Alexander would let her drive if she happened to sit on the front seat of the carry-all; Dr Carr was seldom so tired that he could not tell her a story – and nobody told such nice stories as Dr Carr, Amy thought; Elsie invented all manner of charming games for the hours before bedtime; Clover made wonderful capes and bonnets for Mabel and Maria Matilda; and Katy – Katy did all sorts of things.

Katy had a peculiar gift with children which is not easy to define. Some people possess it, and some do not; it cannot be learned, it comes by nature. She was bright and firm and equable all at once. She both amused and influenced them. There was something about her which excited the childish imagination, and always they felt her sympathy. Amy was a tractable child, and intelligent beyond her age, but she was never quite so good with anyone as with Katy. She followed her about like a little lover; she lavished upon her certain special words and caresses which she gave to no one else; she would kneel on her lap, patting Katy's shoulders with her soft hand, and cooing up into her face like a happy dove, for a half hour together. Katy laughed at these demonstrations, but they pleased her very much. She loved to be loved, as all affectionate people do, but most of all by a child.

At last, the long convalescence ended. Walter was carried away to his father, with every possible precaution against fatigue and exposure, and an army of work-people was turned into Mrs Ashe's house. Plaster was scraped and painted, wallpapers torn down, mattresses made over, and clothing burned. At last Dr Carr pro-nounced the premises in a sanitary condition, and Mrs Ashe sent for her little girl to come home again.

Amy was overjoyed at the prospect of seeing her mother, but at the last moment she clung to Katy and cried as if her heart would break.

'I want you too,' she said. 'Oh, if Dr Carr would only let you come and live with me and mamma, I should be so happy! I shall be so lonely!'

'Nonsense!' cried Clover. 'Lonely with mamma, and those poor children of yours, who have been wondering all these weeks what has become of you! They'll want a great deal of attention at first, I am sure – medicine and new clothes and whippings – all manner of things. You remember I promised to make a dress for Effie Deans out of that blue-and-brown plaid like Johnnie's balmoral. I mean to begin it tomorrow.'

'Oh, will you?' – forgetting her grief – 'that will be lovely. The skirt needn't be *very* full, you know. Effie doesn't walk much, because of only having one leg. She will be *so* pleased, for she hasn't had a new dress since I don't know when.'

Consoled by the prospect of Effie's satisfaction, Amy departed quite cheerfully, and Mrs Ashe was spared the pain of seeing her only child in tears on the first evening of their reunion. But Amy talked so constantly of Katy, and seemed to love her so much, that it put a plan into her mother's head which led to important results, as the next chapter will show.

CHAPTER

2

AN INVITATION

It is a curious fact, and makes life very interesting, that generally speaking, none of us have any expectation that things are going to happen till the very moment when they do happen. We wake up some morning with no idea that a great happiness is at hand, and before night it has come, and all the world is changed for us; or we wake bright and cheerful, with never a guess that clouds of sorrow are lowering in our sky to put all the sunshine out for a while, and before noon all is dark. Nothing whispers of either the joy or the grief. No instinct bids us to delay or to hasten the opening of the letter or telegram, or the lifting of the latch of the door on which stands the messenger of good or ill. And because it may be, and often is, happy tidings that come, and joyful things which happen, each fresh day as it dawns upon us is like an unread story, full of possible interest and adventure, to be made ours as soon as we have cut the pages and begun to read.

Nothing whispered to Katy Carr, as she sat at the window mending a long rent in Johnnie's school coat and saw Mrs Ashe come in at the side gate and ring the office bell, that the visit had any special significance for her. Mrs Ashe often did come to the office to consult Dr Carr. Amy might not be quite well, Katy thought, or there might be a letter with something about Walter in it, or perhaps matters had gone wrong at the house, where paperers and painters were still at work. So she went calmly on with her darning, drawing the 'ravelling' with which her needle was threaded carefully in and out, and taking nice even stitches without one prophetic thrill or tremor; if only she could have looked through the two walls and two doors which separated the room in which she sat from the office, and heard what Mrs Ashe was saying, the school coat would have been thrown to the winds, and for all her tall stature and propriety she would have been skipping with delight and astonishment. For Mrs Ashe was asking papa to let her do the very thing of all others that she most longed to do; she was asking him to let Katy go with her to Europe!

'I am not very well,' she told the doctor. 'I got tired and run down while Walter was ill, and I don't seem to be able to throw it off as I hoped I should. I feel as if a change would do me good. Don't you think so yourself?'

'Yes, I do,' Dr Carr admitted.

'This idea of Europe is not altogether a new one,' continued Mrs Ashe. 'I have always meant to go sometime, and have put it off, partly because I dreaded going alone, and didn't know anybody whom I exactly wanted to take with me. But if you will let me have Katy, Dr Carr, it will settle all my difficulties. Amy loves her dearly, and so do I; she is just the companion I need. If I have her with me, I shan't be afraid of anything. I do hope you will consent.'

'How long do you mean to be away?' asked Dr Carr,

divided between pleasure at these compliments to Katy and dismay at the idea of losing her.

'About a year, I think. My plans are rather vague as yet. But my idea was to spend a few weeks in Scotland and England first – I have some cousins in London who will be good to us, and an old friend of mine married a gentleman who lives on the Isle of Wight; perhaps we might go there. Then we could cross over to France, and visit Paris and a few other places, and before it gets cold, go down to Nice, and from there to Italy. Katy would like to see Italy. Don't you think so?'

'I dare say she would,' said Dr Carr, with a smile. 'She would be a queer girl if she didn't.'

'There is one reason why I thought Italy would be particularly pleasant this winter for me and for her too,' went on Mrs Ashe, 'and that is, because my brother will be there. He is a lieutenant in the navy, you know, and his ship, the *Natchitoches*, is one of the Mediterranean squadron. They will be in Naples by and by, and if we were there at the same time we should have Ned to go about with. He would take us to the receptions on the frigate, and everything, which would be a nice chance for Katy. Then towards spring I should like to go to Florence and Venice, and visit the Italian lakes and Switzerland in the early summer. But all this depends on your letting Katy go. If you decide against it, I shall give the whole thing up. But you won't decide against it' – coaxingly – 'you will be kinder than that. I will take the best possible care of her, and do all I can to make her happy, if only you will consent to lend her to me. I shall consider it *such* a favour. And it is to cost you nothing. You understand, Doctor, she is to be my guest all through. That is a point I want to make clear in the outset; for she goes for my sake, and I cannot take her on any other conditions. Now, Dr Carr, please, please! I am sure you won't deny me, when I have so set my heart upon having her.'

Mrs Ashe was very pretty and persuasive, but still Dr Carr hesitated. To send Katy for a year's pleasuring in Europe was a thing that had never occurred to him as possible. The cost alone would have prevented it, for country doctors with six children are not apt to be rich men, even in the limited and old-fashioned construction of the word 'wealth'. It seemed equally impossible to let her go at Mrs Ashe's expense: at the same time, the chance was such a good one, and Mrs Ashe so much in earnest and so urgent, that it was difficult to refuse point blank. He finally consented to take time for consideration before making his decision.

'I will talk it over with Katy,' he said. 'The child ought to have a say in the matter; and whatever we decide, you must let me thank you in her name as well as my own for your great kindness in proposing it.'

'Doctor, I'm not kind at all, and I don't want to be thanked. My desire to take Katy with me to Europe is purely selfish. I am a lonely person,' she went on, 'I have no mother or sister, and no cousins of my own age. My brother's profession keeps him at sea; I scarcely ever see him. I have no one but a couple of old aunts, too feeble in health to travel with me or to be counted on in case of any emergency. You see, I am a real case for pity.'

Mrs Ashe spoke gaily, but her brown eyes were dim with tears as she ended her little appeal. Dr Carr, who was soft hearted where women were concerned, was touched. Perhaps his face showed it, for Mrs Ashe added in a more hopeful tone:

'But I won't tease any more. I know you will not refuse me unless you think it right and necessary, and,' she continued mischievously, 'I have great faith in Katy as an ally. I am pretty sure that she will say that she wants to go.'

And indeed Katy's cry of delight when the plan was proposed to her said that sufficiently, without need of further explanation. To go to Europe for a year with Mrs Ashe and Amy seemed simply too delightful to be true. All the things she had heard about and read about – cathedrals, pictures, Alpine peaks, famous places, famous people – came rushing into her mind in a sort of bewildering tide as dazzling as it was overwhelming. Dr Carr's objections, his reluctance to part with her, melted before the radiance of her satisfaction. He had no idea that Katy would care so much about it. After all, it was a great chance – perhaps the only one of the sort that she would ever have. Mrs Ashe could well afford to give Katy this treat, he knew, and it was quite true what she said, that it was a favour to her as well as to Katy. This train of reasoning led to its natural results. Dr Carr began to waver in his mind.

But, the first excitement over, Katy's second thoughts were more sober ones. How could Papa manage without her for a whole year? she asked herself. He would miss her, she well knew; and might not the charge of the house be too much for Clover? The preserves were almost all made, that was one comfort, but there were the winter clothes to be seen to; Dorry needed new flannels, Elsie's dresses must be altered for Johnnie; there were cucumbers to pickle, and the coal to order! A host of housewifely cares began to troop through Katy's mind; a little pucker came into her forehead, and a worried look across the face which had been so bright a few minutes before.

Strange to say, it was that little pucker and the look of worry which decided Dr Carr.

'She is only twenty-one,' he reflected, 'hardly out of childhood. I don't want her to settle into an anxious drudging state, and lose her youth with caring for us all. She shall go; though how we are to manage without her I don't see. Little Clover will have to come to the fore, and show what sort of stuff there is in her.'

'Little Clover' came gallantly 'to the fore' when the first shock of the surprise was over, and she had relieved her mind with one long private cry over having to do without Katy for a year. Then she wiped her eyes, and began to revel unselfishly in the idea of her sister having so great a treat. Anything and everything seemed possible to secure it for her, and she made light of all Katy's many anxieties and apprehensions.

'My dear child, I know a flannel undershirt when I see one, just as well as you do,' she declared. 'Tucks in Johnnie's dress, forsooth! Why, of course. Ripping out a tuck doesn't require any superhuman ingenuity! Give me your scissors, and I'll show you at once. Quince marmalade? Debby can make that; hers is about as good as yours. And if it wasn't, what should we care, as long as you are ascending Mont Blanc, and hobnobbing with Michelangelo and the crowned heads of Europe? I'll make the spiced peaches! I'll order the kindling! And if there ever comes a time when I feel lost and can't manage without advice, I'll go across to Mrs Hall. Don't worry about us. We shall get on happily and easily; in fact, I shouldn't be surprised if I developed such a turn for housekeeping, that when you come back the family refused to change, and you had just to sit for the rest of your life and twirl your thumbs and watch me do it! Wouldn't that be fine?' and Clover laughed merrily. 'So, Katy darling, cast that shadow from your brow, and look as a girl ought to look who's going to Europe. Why, if it were I who were going, I should simply stand on my head every moment of the time!'

'Not a very convenient position for packing,' said Katy, smiling.

'Yes it is, if you just turn your trunk upside down! When I think of all the delightful things you are going to do I can hardly sit still. I *love* Mrs Ashe for inviting you.'

'So do I,' said Katy soberly. 'It was the kindest thing. I can't think why she did it.'

'Well, I can,' replied Clover, always ready to defend Katy even against herself. 'She did it because she wanted you, and she wanted you because you are the dearest old thing in the world, and the nicest to have about. You needn't say you're not, for you are! Now, Katy, don't waste another thought on such miserable things as pickles and undershirts. We shall get along perfectly well, I do assure you. Just fix your mind instead on the dome of St Peter's, or try to fancy how you'll feel the first time you step into a gondola or see the Mediterranean. There will be a moment! I feel a forty-horse power of housekeeping developing within me; and what fun it will be to get your letters! We shall fetch out the encyclopaedia and the big atlas and the *History of Modern Europe*, and read all about everything you see and all the places you go to; it will be as good as a lesson in geography and history and political economy all combined, only a great deal more interesting! We shall stick out all over with knowledge before you come back, so this makes it a plain duty to go, if it were only for our sakes.' With these zealous promises, Katy was forced to be content. Indeed, contentment was not difficult with such a prospect of delight before her. When once her little anxieties had been laid aside, the idea of the coming journey grew in pleasantness every moment. Night after night she and papa and the children pored over maps and made out schemes for travel and sightseeing, every one of which was likely to be discarded as soon as the real journey began. But they didn't know that, and it made no real difference. Such schemes are the preliminary joys of travel, and it doesn't signify that they come to nothing after they have served their purpose.

Katy learned a great deal while thus talking over what she was to see and do. She read every scrap she could lay her hands on which related to Rome or Florence or Venice or London. The driest details had a charm for her now that she was likely to see the real places. She went about with scraps of paper in her pocket, on which were written such things as these: 'Forum. When built? By whom built? More than one?' 'What does *Cenacola* mean?' 'Cecilia Metella. Who was she?' 'Find out about Saint Catherine of Sienna.' 'Who was Beatrice Cenci?' How she wished that she had studied harder and more carefully before this wonderful chance came to her! People always wish this when they are starting for Europe, and they wish it more and more after they get there, and realize of what value exact ideas and information and a fuller knowledge of the foreign languages are to all travellers, and how they add to the charm of everything seen, and enhance the ease of everything done.

All Burnet took an interest in Katy's plans, and almost everybody had some sort of advice or help, or some little gift, to offer. Old Mrs Worrett, who, though fatter than ever, still retained the power of locomotion, drove in from Conic Section in her roomy carry-all with a present of a rather obsolete copy of *Murray's Guide*, in faded red covers, which her father had used in his youth, and which she was sure Katy would find convenient; also a bottle of Brown's Jamaica Ginger, in case of seasickness. Debby's sister-in-law brought a bundle of dried chamomile for the same purpose. Someone had told her it was the 'handiest thing in the world to take along with you on them steamboats'. Cecy sent a wonderful old-gold and scarlet contrivance to hang on the wall of the state room. There were pockets for watches, and pockets for medicines, and pockets for handkerchiefs and hairpins – in short, there were pockets for everything. There was a pin cushion with 'Bon Voyage' in rows of shining pins, a bottle of eau de Cologne, a cake of soap, and a hammer and tacks to nail the whole up with. Mrs Hall's gift was a warm and very pretty woollen wrapper of dark blue flannel, with a pair of soft knitted slippers to match. Old Mr Worrett sent a note of advice, recommending Katy to take a quinine pill every day that she was away, never to stay out late, because the dews 'over there' were said to be unwholesome, and on no account to drink a drop of water which had not been boiled.

From Cousin Helen came a delightful travelling bag, light and strong at once, and fitted up with all manner of nice little conveniences. Miss Inches sent a *History of Europe* in five fat volumes, which was so heavy that it had to be left at home. In fact, a good many of Katy's presents had to be left at home, including a bronze paper weight in the shape of a griffin, a large pair of brass screw candlesticks, and an ormolu ink-stand with a pen rest attached, which weighed at least a pound and a half. These Katy laid aside to enjoy after her return. Mrs Ashe and Cousin Helen had both warned her of the inconvenient consequences of weight in baggage, and by their advice she limited herself to a single trunk of moderate size, besides a little flat valise for use in her state room.

Clover's gift was a set of blank books for notes, journals, and so on. In one of these Katy made out a list of 'Things I must see', 'Things I must do', 'Things I would like to see', 'Things I would like to do'. Another she devoted to various shopping addresses which had been given her; for though she did not expect to do any shopping herself, she thought Mrs Ashe might find them useful. Katy's ideas were still so simple and unworldly, and her experience of life so small, that it had not occurred to her how very tantalizing it might be to stand in front of shop windows full of delightful things and not be able to buy any of them. She was accordingly over-powered with surprise, gratitude, and the sense of sudden wealth, when, about a week before the start, her father gave her three little thin strips of paper, which he told her were circular notes, and worth a hundred dollars apiece. He also gave her five English sovereigns.

'Those are for immediate use,' he said. 'Put the notes away carefully, and don't lose them. You had better have them cashed one at a time as you require them. Mrs Ashe will explain how. You will need a gown or so before you come back, and you'll want to buy some photographs and so on, and there will be fees –'

'But, Papa,' protested Katy, opening wide her candid eyes, 'I didn't expect you to give me any money, and I'm afraid you are giving me too much. Do you think you can afford it? Really and truly, I don't want to buy things. I shall see everything, you know, and that's enough.'

Her father only laughed.

'You'll be wiser and greedier before the year is out, my dear,' he replied. 'Three hundred dollars won't go far, as you'll find. But it's all I can spare, and I trust you to keep within it, and not come home with any long bills for me to pay.'

'Papa! I should think not!' cried Katy, with unsophisticated horror.

One very interesting thing was to happen before they sailed, the thought of which helped both Katy and Clover through the last hard days, when the preparations were nearly complete and the family had leisure to feel dull and out of spirits. Katy was to make Rose Red a visit.

Rose had by no means been idle during the three years and a half which had elapsed since they all parted at Hillsover, and since which time the girls had not seen her. In fact, she had made more out of the time than any of the rest of them, for she had been engaged for eighteen months, had married, and was now keeping house near Boston with a little Rose of her own, who, she wrote to Clover, was a perfect angel, and more delicious than words could say! Mrs Ashe had taken passage in the *Spartacus*, sailing from Boston, and it was arranged that Katy should spend the last two days before sailing with Rose, while Mrs Ashe and Amy visited an old aunt in Hingham. To see Rose in her own home, and Rose's husband, and Rose's baby, was only next in interest to seeing Europe. None of the changes in her lot seemed to have changed her particularly, to judge by the letter she sent in reply to Katy's announcing her plans, and her letter ran as follows:

Longwood, 20 September

MY DEAREST CHILD,

Your note made me dance with delight. I stood on my head, waving my heels wildly to the breeze, till Deniston thought I must be taken suddenly mad; but when I explained he did the same. It is too enchanting, the whole of it. I put it at the head of all the nice things that ever happened, except my baby. Write the moment you get this by what train you expect to reach Boston, and when you roll into the station you will behold two forms, one tall and stalwart, the other short and fatsome, waiting for you. They will be those of Deniston and myself. Deniston is not beautiful, but he is good, and he is prepared to *adore* you. The baby is both good and beautiful, and you will adore her. I am neither; but you know all about me, and I always did adore you and always shall. I am going out this moment to the butcher's to order a calf fatted for your special delight; and he shall be slain and made into cutlets the moment I hear from you. My funny little house, which is quite a dear little house too, assumes a new interest in my eyes from the fact that you so soon are to see it. It is somewhat queer, as you might know my house would be, but I think you will like it.

I saw Silvery Mary the other day and told her you were coming. She is the same mouse as ever. I shall ask her and some of the other girls to come out to lunch on one of your days. Goodbye, with a hundred and fifty kisses to Clovy and the rest.

Your loving

ROSE RED.

'She never signs herself Browne, I observe,' said Clover, as she finished the letter.

'Oh, Rose Red Browne would sound too funny! Rose Red she must stay till the end of the chapter; no other name could suit her half so well, and I can't imagine her being called anything else. What fun it will be to see her and little Rose!'

'And Deniston Browne,' put in Clover.

'Somehow I find it rather hard to take in the fact that there is a Deniston Browne,' observed Katy.

'It will be easier after you have seen him, perhaps.'

The last day came, as last days will. Katy's trunk, most carefully and exactly packed by the united efforts of the family, stood in the hall, locked and strapped, not to be opened again till the party reached London. This fact gave it a certain awful interest in the eyes of Phil and Johnnie, and even Elsie gazed upon it with respect. The little valise was also ready, and Dorry, the neat-handed, had painted a red star on both ends of both it and the trunk, that they might be easily picked from among a heap of luggage. He now proceeded to prepare and paste on two square cards, labelled respectively, 'Hold' and 'State room'. Mrs Hall had told them that this was the correct thing to do.

Mrs Ashe had been full of business likewise in putting her house to rights for a family who had rented it for the time of her absence, and Katy and Clover had taken a good many hours from their own preparations to help her. All was done at last, and one bright morning in October, Katy stood on the wharf with her family about her, and a lump in her throat which made it difficult to speak to any of them. She stood so very still, and said so very little, that a bystander not acquainted with the circumstances might have dubbed her 'unfeeling', while the fact was that she was feeling too much!

The first bell rang. Katy kissed everybody quietly and went on board with her father. Her parting from him, hardest of all, took place in the midst of a crowd of people; then he had to leave her, and as the wheels began to revolve she went out on the side deck to have a last glimpse of the home faces. There they were: Elsie crying tumultuously, with her head on papa's coat-sleeve; John laughing, or trying to laugh, with big tears running down her cheeks the while; and brave little Clover waving her handkerchief encouragingly, but with a very sober look on her face. Katy's heart went out to the little group with a sudden passion of regret and yearning. Why had she said she would go? What was all Europe in comparison with what she was leaving? Life was so short, how could she take a whole year out of it to spend away from the people she loved best? If it had been left to her to choose, I think she would have flown back to the shore there and then, and given up the journey. I also think she would have been heartily sorry a little later, had she done so.

But it was not left for her to choose. Already the throb of the engines was growing more regular, and the distance widening between the great boat and the wharf. Gradually the dear faces faded into distance, and after watching till the flutter of Clover's handkerchief became an undistinguishable speck, Katy went to the cabin with a heavy heart. But there were Mrs Ashe and Amy, inclined to be homesick also and in need of cheering, and Katy, as she tried to brighten them, gradually grew bright herself and recovered her hopeful spirits. The sun shone, the lake was a beautiful, dazzling blue, and Katy said to herself: 'After all, a year is not very long, and how happy I am going to be!'

CHAPTER

3

ROSE AND ROSEBUD

Thirty-six hours later the Albany train, running smoothly across the green levels beyond the Mill Dam, brought the travellers to Boston.

Katy looked eagerly from the window for her first glimpse of the city of which she had heard so much. 'Dear little Boston! How nice it is to see it again!' she heard a lady behind her say, but why it should be called 'little Boston' she could not imagine. Seen from the train it looked large, imposing, and very picturesque, after flat Burnet with its one bank down to the edge of the lake. She studied the towers, steeples, and red roofs crowding each other up the slopes of the Tri-Mountain, and the big State House dome crowning all, and made up her mind that she liked the look of it better than any other city she had ever seen.

The train slackened its speed, ran for a few moments between rows of tall, shabby brick walls, and with a long, final screech of its whistle came to a halt in the station. Everyone made a simultaneous rush for the door, and Katy and Mrs Ashe, waiting to collect their books and bags, found themselves wedged into their seats and unable to get out. It was a confusing moment, and not comfortable; such moment never are.

But the discomfort brightened into a sense of relief as, looking out of the window, Katy caught sight of a face exactly opposite, which had evidently caught sight of her – a fresh, pretty face, with light, waving hair, pink cheeks all a-dimple, and eyes which shone with laughter and welcome. It was Rose herself, not a bit changed during the years since they parted. A tall young man stood beside her, who must, of course, be her husband, Deniston Browne.

'There is Rose Red,' cried Katy to Mrs Ashe. 'Oh, doesn't she look dear and natural? Do wait and let me introduce you. I want you to know her.'

But the train had come in a little behind time, and Mrs Ashe was afraid of missing the Hingham boat, so she only took a hasty peep from the window at Rose, pronounced her to look charming, kissed Katy hurriedly, reminded her that they must be on the steamer punctually at twelve o'clock the following Saturday, and was gone, with Amy beside her, so that Katy, following last of all the slow-moving line of passengers, stepped all alone down from the platform into the arms of Rose Red.

'You darling!' was Rose's first greeting. 'I began to think you meant to spend the night in the car, you were so long in getting out. Well, how perfectly lovely this is! Deniston, here is Katy; Katy, this is my husband.'

Rose looked about fifteen as she spoke, and so absurdly young to have a 'husband', that Katy could not help laughing as she shook hands with Deniston, and his own eyes twinkled with fun and evident recognition of the same joke. He was a tall young man, with a pleasant, 'steady' face, and seemed to be infinitely amused, in a quiet way, with everything which his wife said and did.

'Let us make haste and get out of this hole,' went on Rose. 'I can scarcely see for the smoke. Deniston, dear, please find the cab, and have Katy's luggage put on it. I am wild to get her home and exhibit baby before she chews up her new sash or does something else that is dreadful, to spoil her looks. I left her sitting in state, Katy, with all her best clothes on, waiting to be made known to you.'

'My large trunk is to go straight to the steamer,' explained Katy, as she gave her checks to Mr Browne. 'I only want the little one taken out to Longwood, please.'

'Now, this is cosy,' remarked Rose, when they were seated in the cab with Katy's bag at their feet. 'Deniston, my love, I wish you were going out with us. There's a nice little bench here all ready and vacant, which is just suited to a man of your inches. You won't? Well, come in the early train, then. Don't forget. Now, isn't he just as nice as I told you he was?' she demanded, the moment the cab began to move.

'He looks very nice indeed, as far as I can judge in three minutes and a quarter.'

'My dear, it ought not to take anybody of ordinary discernment a minute and a quarter to perceive that he is simply the dearest fellow that ever lived,' said Rose. 'I discovered it three seconds after I first beheld him, and was desperately in love with him before he had fairly finished his first bow after introduction.'

'And was he equally prompt?' asked Katy.

'He says so,' replied Rose, with a pretty blush. 'But then, you know, he could hardly say less after such a frank confession on my part. It is no more than decent of him to make believe, even if it is not true. Now, Katy, look at Boston, and see if you don't *love* it!'

The cab had now turned into Boylston Street, and on the right hand lay the Common, green as summer after the autumn rains, with the elm arches leafy still. Long, slant beams of afternoon sun were filtering through the boughs and falling across the turf and the paths, where people were walking and sitting, and children and babies playing together. It was a delightful scene, and Katy received an impression of space and cheer and air and freshness, which ever after was associated with her recollection of Boston.

Rose was quite satisfied with her raptures as they drove through Charles Street, between the Common and the Public Garden, all ablaze with autumn flowers, and down the length of Beacon Street with the blue bay shining between the handsome houses on the water side. Every vestibule and bay window was gay with potted plants and flower boxes, and a concourse of happy-looking people, on foot, on horseback, and in carriages, was surging to and fro like an equal, prosperous tide, while the sunlight glorified all.

'"Boston shows a soft Venetian side",' quoted Katy, after a while. 'I know now what Mr Lowell meant when he wrote that. I don't believe there is a more beautiful place in the world.'

'Why, of course there isn't,' retorted Rose, who was a most devoted little Bostonian, in spite of the fact that she had lived in Washington nearly all her life. 'I've not seen much beside, to be sure, but that is no matter: I know it is true. It is the dream of my life to come into the city to live. I don't care what part I live in – West End, South End, North End; it's all one to me, so long as it is Boston!'

'But don't you like Longwood?' asked Katy, looking out admiringly at the pretty places set amid vines and shrubberies which they were now passing. 'It looks so very pretty and pleasant.'

'Yes, it's well enough for anyone who has a taste for natural beauties,' replied Rose. 'I haven't; I never had. There is nothing I hate so much as nature! I'm a born townie. I'd rather live in one room over Jordan and Marsh's, and see the world wag past, than be the owner of the most romantic villa that ever was built, wherever it may be situated.'

The cab now turned in at a gate and followed a curving drive bordered with trees to a pretty stone house with a porch embowered with Virginia creepers, before which it stopped.

'Here we are!' cried Rose, springing out. 'Now, Katy, you mustn't even take time to sit down before I show you the dearest baby that ever was sent to this sinful earth. Here, let me take your bag; come straight upstairs, and I will exhibit her to you.'

They ran up accordingly, and Rose took Katy into a large sunny nursery, where, tied with pink ribbons into a little basket chair and watched over by a pretty young nurse, sat a dear, fat, fair baby, so exactly like Rose in miniature that no one could possibly have mistaken the relationship. The baby began to laugh and coo as soon as it caught sight of its gay little mother, and exhibited just such another dimple as hers, in the middle of a pink cheek. Katy was enchanted.

'Oh, you darling!' she said. 'Would she come to me, do you think, Rose?'

'Why, of course she will!' replied Rose, picking up the baby as if she had been a pillow, and stuffing her into

Katy's arms head first. 'Now, just look at her, and tell me if you ever saw anything so enchanting in the whole course of your life before? Isn't she big? Isn't she beautiful? Isn't she good? Just see her little hands and her hair! She never cries except when it is clearly her duty to cry. See her turn her head to look at me! Oh, you angel!' And, seizing the long-suffering baby, she smothered it with kisses. 'I never, never, never did see anything so sweet. Smell her, Katy! Doesn't she smell like heaven?'

Little Rose was indeed a delicious baby, all dimples and good humour and violet powder, with a skin as soft as a lily's leaf, and a happy capacity for allowing herself to be petted and cuddled without remonstrance. Katy wanted to hold her all the time, but this Rose would by no means permit; in fact, I may as well say at once that the two girls spent a great part of their time during the visit in fighting for the possession of the baby, who looked on at the struggle, and smiled on the victor, whichever it happened to be, with all the philosophic composure of Helen of Troy. She was so sunny and equable that it was no more trouble to care for and amuse her than if she had been a bird or a kitten, and, as Rose remarked, it was 'ten times better fun'.

'I was never allowed as many dolls as I wanted in my infancy,' she said. 'I suppose I tore them to pieces too soon.'

'Were you such a very bad child?' asked Katy.

'Oh, utterly depraved, I believe! You wouldn't think so now, would you? I recollect some dreadful occasions at school. Once I had my head pinned up in my apron because I *would* make faces at the other scholars, and they laughed; but I promptly bit a bay window through the apron, and ran my tongue out of it till they laughed worse than ever. The teacher used to send me home with notes fastened to my pinafore with things like this written in them: "Little Frisk has been more troublesome than usual today. She has pinched all the younger children, and bent the bonnets of all the older ones. We hope to see an amendment soon, or we do not know what we shall do."'

'Why did they call you Little Frisk?' inquired Katy, after she had recovered from the laugh which Rose's reminiscences called forth.

'It was a term of endearment, I suppose, but somehow my family never seemed to enjoy it as they ought. I cannot understand,' she went on reflectively, 'why I had not sense enough to suppress those awful little notes. It would have been so easy to lose them on the way home, but somehow it never occurred to me. Little Rose will be wiser than that, won't you, my angel? She will tear up the horrid notes – mammy will show her how!'

All the time that Katy was washing her face and brushing the dust of the railway from her dress, Rose sat by with the little Rose in her lap, entertaining her thus. When she was ready, the droll little mamma tucked her baby under her arm and led the way downstairs to a large square parlour with a bay window, through which the westering sun was shining. It was a pretty room, and had a flavour about it 'just like Rose', Katy declared. No one else would have hung the pictures or looped back the curtains in exactly that way, or have hit upon the happy device of filling the grate with a great bunch of marigolds, pale brown, golden, and orange, to simulate the fire which would have been quite too warm on so mild an evening. Morris papers and chintzes and 'artistic' shades of colour were in their infancy at that date, but Rose's

taste was in advance of her time, and with a foreshadow-
ing of the coming 'reaction', she had chosen a 'greenery,
yallery' paper for her walls, against which hung various
articles which looked a great deal queerer then than they
would today. There was a mandolin, picked up at some
Eastern sale, a warming pan in shining brass from her
mother's attic, two old samplers worked in faded silks,
and a quantity of gaily-tinted Japanese fans and
embroideries. She had also begged from an old aunt at
Beverly Farms a couple of droll little armchairs in white
painted wood, with covers of antique needlework. One
had 'Chit' embroidered on the middle of its cushion, the
other, 'Chat'. These stood suggestively at the corners of
the hearth.

'Now, Katy,' said Rose, seating herself in 'Chit', 'pull
up "Chat", and let us begin.'

So they did begin, and went on, interrupted only by
Baby Rose's coos and splutters till the dusk fell, till
appetizing smells floated through from the rear of the
house, and the click of a latch key announced Mr
Browne, come home just in time for dinner.

The two days' visit went only too quickly. There is
nothing more fascinating to a girl than the *menage* of a
young couple of her own age. It is a sort of playing at real
life without the cares and the sense of responsibility that
real life is sure to bring. Rose was an adventurous housekeeper. She was still new to the position; she found it
very entertaining, and she delighted in experiments of all
sorts. If they turned out well, it was good fun; if not, that
was funnier still! Her husband, for all his serious manner,
had a real boy's love of a lark, and he aided and abetted
her in all sorts of whimsical devices. They owned a dog
who was only less dear than the baby, a cat only less dear

than the dog, a parrot whose education required constant supervision, and a hutch of ring doves whose melancholy little 'whuddering' coos were the delight of Rose. The house seemed astir with young life all over. The only elderly thing in it was the cook, who had the reputation of a dreadful temper; only unfortunately, Rose made her laugh so much that she never found time to be cross.

Katy felt quite an old, experienced person amid all this movement and liveliness and cheer. It seemed to her that nobody in the world could possibly be having such a good time as Rose; but Rose did not take the same view of the situation.

'It's all very well now,' she said, 'while the warm weather lasts, but in winter Longwood is simply gruesome. The wind never stops blowing day or night. It howls and it roars and it screams, till I feel as if every nerve in my body were on the point of snapping in two. And the snow, ugh! And the wind, ugh! And burglars! Every night of our lives they come – or I think they come – and I lie awake and hear them sharpening their tools and forcing the locks and murdering the cook and kidnapping Baby, till I long to die and have done with them forever! O, nature is the most unpleasant thing!'

'Burglars are not nature,' objected Katy.

'What are they, then? Art? High art? Well, whatever they are, I do not like them. Oh, if ever the happy day comes when Deniston consents to move into town, I never wish to set my eyes on the country again as long as I live, unless – well, yes, I should like to come out just once more in the horse-cars and *kick* that elm tree by the fence! The number of times that I have lain awake at night listening to its creaking!'

'You might kick it without waiting to have a house in town.'

'Oh, I shouldn't dare as long as we are living here! You never know what nature may do. She has ways of her own of getting even with people,' remarked her friend, solemnly.

No time must be lost in showing Boston to Katy, Rose said. So, the morning after her arrival she was taken in bright and early to see the sights. There were not quite so many sights to be seen then as there are today. The Art Museum had not got much above its foundations; the new Trinity Church was still in the future; but the big organ and the bronze statue of Beethoven were in their glory, and every day at high noon a small straggling audience wandered into the Music Hall to hear the instrument played. To this extempore concert Katy was taken, and to Faneuil Hall and the Athenaeum, to Doll and Richards, where was an exhibition of pictures, to the Granary Graveyard, and the Old South. Then the girls did a little shopping, and by that time they were quite tired enough to make the idea of luncheon agreeable, so they took the path across the Common to the Joy Street Mall.

Katy was charmed by all she had seen. The delightful nearness of so many interesting things surprised her. She perceived what is one of Boston's chief charms – that the Common and its surrounding streets make a natural centre and rallying point for the whole city, as the heart is the centre of the body and keeps up a quick correspondence and regulates the life of all its extremities. The stately old houses on Beacon Street, with their rounded fronts, deep window casements, and here and there a mauve or a lilac pane set in the sashes, took her fancy greatly, and so did the State House, whose situation made it sufficiently imposing, even before the gilding of the dome.

Up the steep steps of the Joy Street Mall they went, to the house on Mt Vernon Street which the Reddings had taken on their return from Washington nearly three years before. Rose had previously shown Katy the site of the old family house on Summer Street, where she was born, now given over wholly to warehouses and shops. Their present residence was one of those wide, old-fashioned brick houses on the crest of the hill, whose upper windows command the view across to the Boston Highlands; in the rear was a spacious yard, almost large enough to be called a garden, walled in with ivies and grape-vines, under which were long beds full of roses and chrysanthemums and marigolds and mignonette.

Rose carried a latch key in her pocket, which she said had been one of her wedding gifts; with this she unlocked the front door and let Katy into a roomy, white-painted hall.

'We will go straight through to the back steps,' she said. 'Mammy is sure to be sitting there. She always sits there till the first frost; she says it makes her think of the country. How different people are! I don't want to think of the country, but I'm never allowed to forget it for a moment. Mamma is so fond of those steps and the garden.'

There, to be sure, Mrs Redding was found sitting in a wickerwork chair under the shade of the grapevines, with a basket of mending at her side. It looked so homely and country-like to find a person thus occupied in the middle of a busy city that Katy's heart warmed to her at once.

Mrs Redding was a fair little woman, scarcely taller than Rose and very much like her. She gave Katy a kind welcome.

'You do not seem like a stranger,' she said. 'Rose has told us so much about you and your sister. Sylvia will be very disappointed not to see you. She went off to make some visits when we broke up in the country, and is not to be home for three weeks yet.'

Katy was disappointed too, for she had heard a great deal about Sylvia and had wished very much to meet her. She was shown her picture, from which she gathered that she did not look in the least like Rose; for, though equally fair, her fairness was of the tall aquiline type, quite different from Rose's dimpled prettiness. In fact, Rose resembled her mother, and Sylvia her father; they were only alike in little peculiarities of voice and manner, of which a portrait did not enable Katy to judge.

The two girls had a cosy little luncheon with Mrs Redding, after which Rose carried Katy off to see the house and everything in it which was in any way connected with her own personal history – the room where she used to sleep, the high chair in which she sat as a baby and which was presently to be made over to little Rose, the sofa where Deniston offered himself, and the exact spot on the carpet on which she had stood while they were being married! Last of all –

'Now you shall see the best and dearest thing in the whole house,' she said, opening the door of a room on the second storey. 'Grandmamma, here is my friend Katy Carr, whom you have so often heard me tell about.'

It was a large, pleasant room, with a little wood fire blazing in a grate, by which, in an armchair full of cushions, with a solitaire board on a little table beside her, sat a sweet old lady. This was Rose's father's mother. She was nearly eighty, but she was beautiful still, and her manner had a gracious old-fashioned courtesy which was full of charm. She had been thrown from a carriage the year before, and had never since been able to come downstairs or to mingle in the family life.

'They come to me instead,' she told Katy. 'There is no lack of pleasant company,' she added; 'everyone is very good to me. I have a reader for two hours a day, and I read to myself a little, and play patience and solitaire, and never lack entertainment.'

There was something restful in the sight of such a lovely specimen of old age. Katy realized, as she looked at her, what a loss it had been to her own life that she had never known either of her grandparents. She sat and gazed at old Mrs Redding with a mixture of regret and fascination. She longed to hold her hand, and kiss her, and play with her beautiful silvery hair, as Rose did. Rose was evidently the old lady's peculiar darling. They were on the most intimate terms, and Rose dimpled and twinkled, and made saucy speeches, and told all her little adventures and the baby's achievements, and made jests and talked nonsense, as freely as to a person of her own age. It was a delightful relation.

'Grandmamma has taken a fancy to you, I can see,' she told Katy, as they drove back to Longwood. 'She always wants to know my friends, and she has her own opinions about them, I can tell you.'

'Do you really think she liked me?' said Katy warmly. 'I am so glad if she did, for I *loved* her. I never saw a really beautiful old person before.'

'Oh, there's nobody like her!' rejoined Rose. 'I can't

imagine what it would be not to have her.' Her merry little face was quite sad and serious as she spoke. 'I wish she were not so old,' she added, with a sigh. 'If we could only put her back twenty years! Then, perhaps, she would live as long as I do.'

But, alas! there is no putting back the hands on the dial of time, no matter how much we may desire it.

The second day of Katy's visit was devoted to the luncheon party of which Rose had written in her letter, and which was meant to be a reunion or 'side chapter' of the SSUC. Rose had asked every old Hillsover girl who was within reach. There was Mary Silver, of course, and Esther Dearborn, both of whom lived in Boston; and by good luck Alice Gibbons happened to be making Esther a visit, and Ellen Gray came in from Waltham, where her father had recently been settled over a parish, so that altogether they made six of the original nine of the society. Quaker Row itself never heard a merrier confusion of tongues than resounded through Rose's pretty parlour for the first hour after the arrival of the guests.

There was everybody to ask after, and everything to tell. The girls all seemed wonderfully unchanged to Katy, but they professed to find her very grown up and dignified.

'I wonder if I am?' she said. 'Clover never told me so. But perhaps she has grown dignified too.'

'Nonsense!' cried Rose; 'Clover could no more be dignified than my baby could. Mary Silver, give me that child this moment! I never saw such a greedy thing as you are; you have kept her to yourself at least a quarter of an hour, and it isn't fair.'

'Oh, I beg your pardon!' said Mary, laughing and

covering her mouth with her hand exactly in her old, shy, half-frightened way.

'We only need Mrs Nipson to make our little party complete,' went on Rose, 'or dear Miss Jane! What has become of Miss Jane, by the way? Do any of you know?'

'Oh, she is still teaching at Hillsover and waiting for her missionary! He has never come back. Berry Searles says that when he goes out to walk he always walks away from the United States, for fear of diminishing the distance between them.'

'What a shame!' said Katy, though she could not help laughing. 'Miss Jane was really quite nice – no, not *nice* exactly – but she had good things about her.'

'Had she?' remarked Rose satirically. 'I never observed them. It required eyes like yours, real "double million magnifying glasses of h'extra power", to find them out. She was all teeth and talons as far as I was concerned; but I think she really did have a softish spot in her old heart for you, Katy, and it's the only good thing I ever knew about her.'

'What has become of Lilly Page?' asked Ellen.

'She's in Europe with her mother. I dare say you'll meet, Katy, and what a pleasure that will be! And have you heard about Bella? She's teaching school in the Indian Territory. Just fancy that scrap teaching school!'

'Isn't it dangerous?' asked Mary Silver.

'Dangerous! How? To her scholars, do you mean? Oh, the Indians! Well, her scalp will be easy to identify if she has adhered to her favourite pomatum; that's one comfort,' put in naughty Rose.

It was a merry luncheon indeed, as little Rose seemed to think, for she laughed and cooed incessantly. The girls were enchanted with her, and voted her by acclamation an honorary member of the SSUC. Her health was drunk in Apollinaris water with all the honours, and Rose returned thanks in a droll speech. The friends told each other their histories for the past three years, but it was curious how little, on the whole, most of them had to tell. Though, perhaps, that was because they did not tell all; for Alice Gibbons confided to Katy in a whisper that they strongly suspected Esther of being engaged, and at the same moment Ellen Gray was convulsing Rose by the intelligence that a theological student from Andover was being 'very attentive' to Mary Silver.

'My dear, I don't believe it,' Rose said, 'not even a theological student would dare, and if he did, I am quite sure Mary would consider it most improper. You must be mistaken, Ellen.'

'No, I'm not mistaken, for the theological student is my second cousin, and his sister told me all about it. They are not engaged exactly, but she hasn't said no; so he hopes she will say yes.'

'Oh, she'll never say no, but then she will never say yes, either! He would better take silence as consent! Well, I never did think I should live to see Silvery Mary married. I should as soon have expected to find the Thirty-Nine Articles engaged in a flirtation. She's a dear old thing, though, and as good as gold, and I shall consider second cousin a lucky man if he persuades her.'

'I wonder where we shall all be when you come back, Katy,' said Esther Dearborn, as they parted at the gate. 'A year is a long time; all sorts of things may happen in a year.'

These words rang in Katy's ears as she fell asleep that night. 'All sorts of things may happen in a year,' she thought, 'and they may not be all happy things, either.'

Almost she wished that the journey to Europe had never been thought of!

But when she woke the next morning to the brightest of October suns shining out of a clear blue sky, her misgivings fled. There could not have been a more beautiful day for their start.

She and Rose went early into town, for old Mrs Redding had made Katy promise to come for a few minutes to say goodbye. They found her sitting by the fire as usual, though her windows were open to admit the sun-warmed air. A little basket of grapes stood on the table beside her, with a nosegay of tea-roses on top. These were from Rose's mother, for Katy to take on board the steamer; and there was something else, a small parcel twisted up in thin white paper.

'It is my goodbye gift,' said the dear old lady. 'Don't open it now. Keep it till you are well out at sea, and get some little thing with it as a keepsake from me.'

Grateful and wondering, Katy put the little parcel in her pocket. With kisses and good wishes she parted from these new-made friends, and she and Rose drove to the steamer, stopping for Mr Browne by the way. They were a little late, so there was not much time for farewells after they arrived, but Rose snatched a moment for a private interview with the stewardess, unnoticed by Katy, who was busy with Mrs Ashe and Amy.

The bell rang, and the great steam vessel slowly backed into the stream. Then her head was turned to sea, and down the bay she went, leaving Rose and her husband still waving their handkerchiefs on the pier. Katy watched them to the last, and when she could no longer distinguish them, felt that her final link with home was broken.

It was not until she had settled her things in the little cabin which was to be her home for the next ten days, had put her bonnet and dress for safe keeping in the upper berth, nailed up her red and yellow bag, and donned the woollen gown, ulster, and soft felt hat which were to do service during the voyage, that she found time to examine the mysterious parcel.

Behold, it was a large, beautiful gold piece, worth twenty dollars!

'What a darling old lady!' said Katy, and she gave the gold piece a kiss. 'How did she come to think of such a thing? I wonder if there is anything in Europe good enough to buy with it?'

CHAPTER
4
ON THE *SPARTACUS*

The ulster and the felt hat soon came off again, for a head wind lay waiting in the offing, and the *Spartacus* began to pitch and toss in a manner which made all her unseasoned passengers glad to betake themselves to their berths. Mrs Ashe and Amy were among the earliest victims of seasickness, and Katy, after helping them to settle in their state rooms, found herself too dizzy and ill to sit up a moment longer, and thankfully resorted to her own.

As the night came on, the wind grew stronger and the motion worse. The *Spartacus* had the reputation of being a dreadful 'roller', and seemed bound to justify it on this particular voyage. Down, down, down the great hull would slide till Katy would hold her breath with fear lest it might never right itself again; then slowly, slowly the turn would be made, and up, up, up it would go, till the list on the other side was equally alarming. On the whole, Katy preferred to have her own side of the ship the downward one, for it was less difficult to keep herself in the berth, from which she was in continual danger of being thrown. The night seemed endless, for she was too frightened to sleep except in broken snatches, and when day dawned, and she looked through the little round pane of glass in the port hole, only grey sky and grey weltering waves and flying spray and rain met her view.

'Oh, dear, why do people ever go to sea, unless they must?' she thought feebly to herself. She wanted to get up and see how Mrs Ashe had lived through the night, but the attempt to move made her so miserably ill that she was glad to sink again on her pillows.

The stewardess looked in with offers of tea and toast, the very idea of which was simply dreadful, and pronounced the other lady ''orribly ill, worse than you are, Miss,' and the little girl 'takin' on dreadful in the h'upper berth'. Of this fact Katy soon had audible proof, for as her dizzy senses rallied a little, she could hear Amy in the opposite state room crying and sobbing pitifully. She seemed to be angry as well as sick, for she was scolding her poor mother in the most vehement fashion.

'I hate being at sea,' Katy heard her say. 'I won't stay in this nasty old ship. Mamma! Mamma! Do you hear me? I won't stay in this ship! It wasn't a bit kind of you to bring me to such a horrid place. It was very unkind; it was cruel. I want to go back, Mamma. Tell the captain to take me back to the land. Mamma, why don't you speak to me? Oh, I am so sick and so very unhappy! Don't you wish you were dead? I do!'

And then came another storm of sobs, but never a sound from Mrs Ashe, who, Katy suspected, was too ill to speak. She felt very sorry for poor little Amy, raging there in her high berth like some imprisoned creature, but she was powerless to help her. She could only resign herself to her own discomforts, and try to believe that somehow, sometime, this state of things must mend; either they should all get to land or all go to the bottom and be drowned, and at that moment she didn't care very much which it turned out to be.

The gale increased as the day wore on, and the vessel pitched dreadfully. Twice Katy was thrown out of her berth on the floor; then the stewardess came and fixed a sort of movable side to the berth, which held her in, but made her feel like a child fastened into a railed crib. At intervals she could still hear Amy crying and scolding her mother, and conjectured that they were having a dreadful time of it in the other state room. It was all like a bad dream. 'And they call this travelling for pleasure!' thought poor Katy.

One droll thing happened in the course of the second night – at least it seemed droll afterward; at the time Katy was too uncomfortable to enjoy it. Amid the rush of the wind, the creaking of the ship's timbers, and the shrill buzz of the screw, she heard a sound of queer little footsteps in the entry outside of her open door, hopping and leaping together in an odd irregular way, like a regiment of mice or toy soldiers. Nearer and nearer they came, and Katy, opening her eyes, saw a procession of boots and shoes of all sizes and shapes which had evidently been left on the floors or at the doors of various state rooms, and which, in obedience to the lurchings of the vessel, had collected in the cabin. They now seemed to be acting in concert with one another, and really looked alive as they bumped and trotted side by side, and two by two, in at the door and up close to her bedside. There they remained for several moments executing what looked like a dance; then the leading shoe turned on its heel as if giving a signal to the others, and they all

hopped slowly again into the passage way and disappeared. It was exactly like one of Hans Christian
Andersen's fairy tales, Katy wrote to Clover afterward.
She heard them going down the cabin, but how it ended,
or whether the owners of the boots and shoes ever got
their own particular pairs again, she never knew.

Toward morning the gale abated, the sea became
smoother, and she dropped asleep. When she woke the
sun was struggling through the clouds, and she felt
better.

The stewardess opened the port hole to freshen the air,
and helped her to wash her face and smooth her tangled
hair; then she produced a little basin of gruel and a
triangular piece of toast, and Katy found that her appetite
was come again and she could eat.

'And 'ere's a letter, ma'am, which has come for you by
post this morning,' said the nice old stewardess, produc-
ing an envelope from her pocket, and eyeing her patient
with great satisfaction.

'By post!' cried Katy in amazement, 'why, how can that
be?' Then, catching sight of Rose's handwriting on
the envelope, she understood, and smiled at her own
simplicity.

The stewardess beamed at her as she opened it, then
said again, 'Yes, m'm, by post, m'm,' withdrew, and left
Katy to enjoy the little surprise.

The letter was not long, but it was very like its writer.
Rose drew a picture of what Katy would probably be
doing at the time it reached her – a picture so near the
truth that Katy felt as if Rose must have the spirit of
prophecy, especially as she kindly illustrated the situation with a series of pen-and-ink drawings, in which
Katy was depicted as prone in her berth, refusing with

horror to go to dinner, looking longingly backward to-ward the quarter where the United States was supposed to be, and fishing out of her port hole with a crooked pin in hopes of grappling the submarine cable and sending a message to her family to come out at once and take her home. It ended with this short 'poem', over which Katy laughed till Mrs Ashe called feebly across the entry to ask what *was* the matter?

> Break, break, break,
>   And misbehave, O sea,
> And I wish that my tongue could utter
>   The hatred I feel for thee!
>
> Oh, well for the fisherman's child
>   On the sandy beach at his play;
> Oh, well for all sensible folk
>   Who are safe at home today!
>
> But this horrible ship keeps on,
>   And is never a moment still,
> And I yearn for the touch of the nice dry land,
>   Where I needn't feel so ill!
>
> Break! break! break!
>   There is no good left in me;
> For the dinner I ate on the shore so late
>   Has vanished into the sea!

Laughter is very restorative after the forlornness of seasickness, and Katy was so stimulated by her letter that she managed to struggle into her dressing gown and slippers and across the entry to Mrs Ashe's state room. Amy had fallen asleep at last and must not be woken up, so their interview was conducted in whispers. Mrs Ashe had by no means got to the tea-and-toast stage yet, and was feeling miserable enough.

'I have had the most dreadful time with Amy,' she said. 'All day yesterday, when she wasn't sick, she was raging at me from the upper berth, and I too ill to say a word in reply. I never knew her so naughty! And it seemed very neglectful not to come to see after you, poor dear child, but really I couldn't raise my head!'

'Neither could I, and I felt just as guilty not to be taking care of you,' said Katy. 'Well, the worst is over with all of us, I hope. The vessel doesn't pitch half so much now, and the stewardess says we shall feel a great deal better as soon as we get on deck. She is coming presently to help me up, and when Amy wakes, won't you let her be dressed, and I will take care of her while Mrs Barrett attends to you.'

'I don't think I can be dressed,' sighed poor Mrs Ashe. 'I feel as if I should just lie here till we get to Liverpool.'

'Oh, no, h'indeed, mum – no, you won't,' put in Mrs Barrett, who at that moment appeared, gruel cup in hand. 'I don't never let my ladies lie in their berths a moment longer than there is need of. I h'always get them on deck as soon as possible to get the h'air. It's the best medicine you can 'ave, ma'am, the fres h'air, h'indeed it h'is.'

Stewardesses are all powerful on board ship, and Mrs Barrett was so persuasive and positive that it was not possible to resist her. She got Katy into her dress and wraps, and seated her on deck in a chair with a great rug wrapped about her feet, with very little effort on Katy's part. Then she dived down the companion way again, and in the course of an hour appeared escorting a big, burly steward, who carried poor little pale Amy in his arms as easily as though she had been a kitten. Amy gave a scream of joy at the sight of Katy, and cuddled down in her lap under the warm rug with a sigh of relief and satisfaction.

'I thought I was never going to see you again,' she said, with a little squeeze. 'Oh, Miss Katy, it has been so horrid! I never thought that going to Europe meant such dreadful things as this!'

'This is only the beginning; we shall get across the sea in a few days, and then we shall find out what going to Europe really means. But what made you believe so, Amy, and cry and scold poor mamma when she was sick? I could hear you all the way across the entry.'

'Could you? Then why didn't you come to me?'

'I wanted to, but I was sick too, so sick that I couldn't move. But why were you so naughty? – you didn't tell me.'

'I didn't mean to be naughty, but I couldn't help crying. You would have cried too, and so would Johnnie, if you had been cooped up in a dreadful old berth at the top of the wall that you couldn't get out of, and hadn't had anything to eat, and nobody to bring you any water when you wanted some. And mamma wouldn't answer when I called to her.'

'She couldn't answer; she was too ill,' explained Katy. 'Well, my pet, it *was* pretty hard for you. I hope we shan't have any more such days. The sea is a great deal smoother now.'

'Mabel looks quite pale; she was sick too,' said Amy, regarding the doll in her arms with an anxious air. 'I hope the fresh h'air will do her good.'

'Is she going to have any fresh hair?' asked Katy, wilfully misunderstanding.

'That was what that woman called it – the fat one who made me come up here. But I'm glad she did, for I feel heaps better already; only I keep thinking of poor little Maria Matilda shut up in the trunk in that dark place, and wondering if she's sick. There's nobody to explain to her down there.'

'They say that you don't feel the motion half so much in the bottom of the ship,' said Katy. 'Perhaps she hasn't noticed it at all. Dear me, how good something smells! I wish they would bring us something to eat.'

A good many passengers had come up by this time, and Robert, the deck steward, was going about, tray in hand, taking orders for lunch. Amy and Katy both felt suddenly ravenous, and when Mrs Ashe, a while later, was helped up the stairs, she was amazed to find them eating cold beef and roasted potatoes, with the finest appetites in the world. 'They had served out their apprenticeships,' the kindly old captain told them, 'and were part of the nautical guild from that time on.' So it proved, for after these two bad days none of the party were sick again during the voyage.

Amy had a clamorous appetite for stories as well as for cold beef, and to appease this craving, Katy started a sort of ocean serial called 'The History of Violet and Emma', which she meant to make last till they got to Liverpool, but which in reality lasted much longer. It might, with equal propriety, have been called 'The Adventures of Two Little Girls Who Didn't Have Any Adventures', for nothing in particular happened to either Emma or Violet during the whole course of their long-drawn-out history. Amy, however, found them perfectly enchanting, and was never weary of hearing how they went to school and came home again, how they got into scrapes and got out of them, how they made good resolutions and broke them, about their Christmas presents and birthday treats, and what they said and how they felt. The first instalment of this unexciting romance was given that first afternoon on deck, and after that Amy claimed a new chapter daily, and it was a chief ingredient of her pleasure during that long sea voyage.

On the third morning Katy woke and dressed so early that she gained the deck before the sailors had finished their scrubbing and holystoning. She took refuge within the companion way, and sat down on the top step of the ladder, to wait till the deck was dry enough to venture upon it. There the Captain found her and drew near for a talk.

Captain Bryce was exactly the kind of sea captain that is found in story books, but not always in real life. He was stout, and grizzled, and brown, and kind. He had a bluff, weather-beaten face, lit up with a pair of shrewd blue eyes which twinkled when he was pleased, and his manner, though it was full of the habit of command, was quiet and pleasant. He was a martinet on board his ship. Not a sailor under him would have dared dispute his orders for a moment, but he was very popular with them, notwithstanding; they liked him as much as they feared him, for they knew him to be their best friend if it came to sickness or trouble with any of them.

Katy and he grew quite intimate during their long morning talk. The Captain liked girls. He had one of his own, about Katy's age, and was fond of talking about her. Lucy was his mainstay at home, he told Katy. Her mother had been 'weakly' now this long time back, and Bess and Nanny were but children yet, so Lucy had to take command and keep things shipshape when he was away.

'She'll be on the look-out when the steamer comes in,'

said the Captain. 'There's a signal we've arranged which means "All's well", and when we get up the river a little way I always look to see if it's flying. It's a bit of a towel hung from a particular window, and when I see it I say to myself, "Thank God! another voyage safely done and no harm come of it." It's a sad kind of work for a man to go off for a twenty-four days' cruise leaving a sick wife on shore behind him. If it wasn't that I have Lucy to look after things, I should have thrown up my command long ago.'

'Indeed, I am glad you have Lucy; she must be a great comfort to you,' said Katy, sympathetically, for the Captain's hearty voice trembled a little as he spoke. She made him tell her the colour of Lucy's hair and eyes, and exactly how tall she was, and what she had studied, and what sort of books she liked. She seemed such a very nice girl, and Katy thought she should like to know her.

The deck had dried fast in the fresh sea wind, and the Captain had just arranged Katy in her chair, and was wrapping the rug about her feet in a fatherly way, when Mrs Barrett, all smiles, appeared from below.

'Oh, 'ere you h'are, miss. I couldn't think what 'ad come to you so early; and you're looking ever so well again, I'm pleased to see. 'Ere's a bundle just arrived, miss, by the parcels delivery.'

'What!' cried simple Katy. Then she laughed at her own foolishness, and took the 'bundle', which was directed in Rose's unmistakable hand.

It contained a pretty little green-bound copy of Emerson's *Poems*, with Katy's name and 'To be read at sea' written on the flyleaf. Somehow, the little gift seemed to bridge the long misty distance which stretched between the vessel's stern and Boston Bay, and to bring home and friends a great deal nearer. With a half-happy, half-tearful pleasure Katy recognized the fact that distance counts for little if people love one another, and that hearts have a telegraph of their own whose messages are as sure and swift as any of those sent over the material lines which link continent to continent and shore with shore.

Later in the morning, Katy, going down to her state room for something, came across a pallid, exhausted-looking lady who lay stretched on one of the long sofas in the cabin; she had a baby in her arms and a little girl sitting at her feet, quite still, with a pair of small hands folded in her lap. The little girl did not seem to be more than four years old. She had two pigtails of thick flaxen hair hanging over her shoulders, and at Katy's approach raised a pair of solemn blue eyes, which had so much appeal in them, though she said nothing, that Katy stopped at once.

'Can I do anything for you?' she asked. 'I am afraid you have been very ill.'

At the sound of her voice the lady on the sofa opened her eyes. She tried to speak, but to Katy's dismay began to cry instead, and when the words came they were strangled with sobs.

'You are so kin-d to ask,' she said. 'If you would give my little girl something to eat! She has had nothing since yesterday, and I have been so ill, and nobody has c-ome near us!'

'Oh!' cried Katy, with horror, 'nothing to eat since yesterday! How did it happen?'

'Everybody has been sick on our side of the ship,' explained the poor lady, 'and I suppose the stewardess thought, as I had a maid with me, that I needed her less than the others. But my maid has been sick too, and oh, so selfish! She wouldn't even take the baby into the berth with her, and I have had all I could do to manage with him, when I couldn't lift up my head. Little Gretchen has had to go without anything, and she has been so good and patient!'

Katy lost no time, but ran for Mrs Barrett, whose indignation knew no bounds when she heard how the helpless party had been neglected.

'It's a new person that stewardess h'is, ma'am,' she explained, 'and most h'inefficient! I told the Captain when she come aboard that I didn't 'ave much opinion of her, and now he'll see how it h'is. I'm h'ashamed that such a thing should 'appen on the *Spartacus*, ma'am – I h'am, h'indeed. H'it never would 'ave been so h'under h'Eliza, ma'am – she's the one that went h'off and got herself married the trip before last, and this person came to take her place.'

All the time that she talked Mrs Barrett was busy in making Mrs Ware – for that, it seemed, was the sick lady's name – more comfortable, and Katy was feeding Gretchen out of a big bowl full of bread and milk which one of the stewards had brought. The little uncomplaining thing was evidently half starved, but with the mouthfuls the pink began to steal back into her cheeks and lips, and the dark circles lessened under the blue eyes. By the time the bottom of the bowl was reached she could smile, but still she said not a word except a whispered *danke schön*. Her mother explained that she had been born in Germany, and always had till now been cared for by a German nurse, so that she knew that language better than English.

Gretchen was a great amusement to Katy and Amy during the rest of the voyage. They kept her on deck with them a great deal, and she was perfectly content with them and very good, though always solemn and quiet. Pleasant people turned up among the passengers, as always happens on an ocean steamship, and others not so pleasant, perhaps, who were rather curious and interesting to watch.

Katy grew to feel as if she knew a great deal about her fellow travellers as time went on. There was the young girl going out to join her parents under the care of a severe governess, whom everybody on board rather pitied. There was the other girl on her way to study art, who was travelling quite alone, and seemed to have nobody to meet her or to go to except a fellow student of her own age, already in Paris; but she seemed quite unconscious of her lonely position, and was competent to grapple with anything or anybody. There was the queer old gentleman who had 'crossed' eleven times before, and had advice and experience to spare for anyone who would listen to them; and the other gentleman, not so old but even more queer, who had 'frozen his stomach', eight years before, by indulging, on a hot summer's day, in sixteen successive ice creams, alternated with ten glasses of equally cold soda water, and who related this exciting experience in turn to everybody on board. There was the bad little boy, whose parents were powerless to oppose him, and who carried terror to the hearts of all beholders whenever he appeared, and the pretty widow who filled the role of reigning belle; and the other widow, not quite so pretty or so much a belle, who had a good deal to say, in a voice made discreetly low, about the activities of her competitor. A great sea-going steamer is a little world in itself, and gives one a glimpse of all sorts and conditions of people and characters.

On the whole, there was no one on the *Spartacus* whom Katy liked so well as sedate little Gretchen except the dear old Captain, with whom she was a prime favourite. He gave Mrs Ashe and herself the seats next to him at table, looked after their comfort in every possible way, and each night at dinner sent Katy one of the apple dumplings made specially for him by the cook, who had gone many voyages with the Captain and knew his fancies. Katy did not care particularly for the dumpling, but she valued it as a mark of regard, and always ate it when she could.

Meanwhile, every morning brought a fresh surprise from that dear, painstaking Rose, who had evidently worked hard and thought harder in contriving pleasures for Katy's first voyage at sea. Mrs Barrett was enlisted in the plot, there could be no doubt of that, and enjoyed the joke as much as anyone, as she presented herself each day with the invariable formula, 'A letter for you, ma'am,' or 'A bundle, miss, come by the Parcels Delivery'. On the fourth morning it was a photograph of Baby Rose, in a little flat morocco case. The fifth brought a wonderful epistle, full of startling pieces of news, none of them true. On the sixth appeared a long, narrow box containing a fountain pen. Then came Mr Howell's *A Foregone Conclusion*, which Katy had never seen; then a box of quinine pills; then a sachet for her trunk; then another burlesque poem; and last of all, a cake of delicious violet soap, 'to wash the sea smell from her hands', the label said. It grew to be one of the little excitements of ship life to watch for the arrival of these daily gifts, and 'What did the mail bring for you this time, Miss Carr?'

was a question frequently asked. Each arrival Katy thought must be the final one, but Rose's forethought had gone so far even as to provide an extra parcel in case the voyage was a day longer than usual, and 'Miss Carr's mail' continued to come in till the very last morning.

Katy never forgot the thrill that went through her when, after so many days of sea, her eyes first caught sight of the dim line of the Irish coast. An exciting and interesting day followed as, after stopping at Queenstown to leave the mails, they sped north-eastward between shores which grew more distinct and beautiful with every hour – on one side Ireland, on the other the bold mountain lines of the Welsh coast. It was late afternoon when they entered the Mersey, and dusk had fallen before the Captain got out his glass to look for the white, fluttering speck in his own window which meant so much to him. Long he studied before he made quite sure that it was there. At last he shut the glass with a satisfied air.

'It's all right,' he said to Katy, who stood near, almost as much interested as he. 'Lucy never forgets, bless her! Well, there's another voyage over and done with, thank God, and my Mary is where she was. It's a load taken from my mind.'

The moon had risen and was shining softly on the river as the crowded tender landed the passengers from the *Spartacus* at the Liverpool docks.

'We shall meet again in London or in Paris,' said one to another, and cards and addresses were exchanged. Then, after a brief delay at the Custom House they separated, each to his own particular destination; and as a general thing, none of them ever saw any of the others again. It is often thus with those who have been fellow voyagers at sea, and it is always a surprise and perplexity to inexperienced travellers that it can be so, and that those who have been so much to each other for ten days can melt away into space and disappear as though the brief intimacy had never existed.

'Four-wheeler or hansom, ma'am?' said a porter to Mrs Ashe.

'Which, Katy?'

'Oh, let us have a hansom! I never saw one, and they look so nice in *Punch*.'

So a hansom cab was called, the two ladies got in, Amy cuddled down between them, the folding doors were shut over their knees like a lap robe, and away they drove up the solidly-paved streets to the hotel where they were to pass the night. It was too late to see or do anything but enjoy the sense of being on firm land once more.

'How lovely it will be to sleep in a bed that doesn't tip or roll from side to side!' said Mrs Ashe.

'Yes, and that is wide enough and long enough and soft enough to be comfortable!' replied Katy. 'I feel as if I could sleep for a fortnight to make up for the bad nights at sea.'

Everything seemed delightful to her – the space for undressing, the great tub of fresh water which stood beside the English-looking wash stand with its ample basin and ewer, the chintz-curtained bed, the coolness, the silence – and she closed her eyes with the pleasant thought it her mind, 'It is really England, and we are really here!'

CHAPTER
5

STORY-BOOK ENGLAND

'Oh, is it raining?' was Katy's first question next morning, when the maid came to call her. The pretty room, with its gaily-flowered chintz, and china, and its brass bedstead, did not look half so bright as when lit with gas the night before, and a dim grey light struggled in at the window, which in America would certainly have meant bad weather coming or already come.

'Oh, no, h'indeed, ma'am, it's a very fine day – not bright, ma'am, but very dry,' was the answer.

Katy couldn't imagine what the maid meant, when she peeped between the curtains and saw a thick dull mist lying over everything, and the pavements opposite her window shining with wet. Afterwards, when she understood better the peculiarities of the English climate, she too learned to call days not absolutely rainy 'fine', and to be grateful for them; but on that first morning her sensations were of bewildered surprise, almost vexation.

Mrs Ashe and Amy were waiting in the coffee room when she went in search of them.

'What shall we have for breakfast,' asked Mrs Ashe – 'our first meal in England? Katy, you order it.'

'Let's have all the things we have read about in books and don't have at home,' said Katy eagerly. But when she came to look over the bill of fare there didn't seem to be many such things. Soles and muffins she finally decided upon, and, as an afterthought, gooseberry jam.

'Muffins sound so very good in Dickens, you know,' she explained to Mrs Ashe, 'and I never saw a sole.'

The soles when they came proved to be nice little pan fish, not unlike what in New England are called 'scup'. All the party took kindly to them, but the muffins were a great disappointment, tough and tasteless, with a flavour about them as of scorched flannel.

'How queer and disagreeable they are!' said Katy. 'I feel as if I were eating rounds cut from an old ironing blanket and buttered! Dear me! What did Dickens mean by making such a fuss about them, I wonder? And I don't care for gooseberry jam, either; it isn't half as good as the jams we have at home. Books are very deceptive.'

'I am afraid they are. We must make up our minds to find a great many things not quite so nice as they sound when we read about them,' replied Mrs Ashe.

Mabel was breakfasting with them, of course, and was heard to remark at this juncture that she didn't like muffins either, and would a great deal rather have waffles; whereupon Amy reproved her, and explained that nobody in England knew what waffles were, they were such a stupid nation, and that Mabel must learn to eat whatever was given her and not find fault with it!

After this moral lesson it was found to be dangerously near train-time, and they all hurried to the station, which, fortunately, was close by. There was rather a scramble and confusion for a few moments, for Katy, who had undertaken to buy the tickets, was puzzled by the unaccustomed coinage, and Mrs Ashe, whose part was to see after the luggage, found herself perplexed and worried by the absence of checks, and by no means disposed to accept the porter's statement, that if she'd only bear in mind that the trunks were in the second van from the engine, and get out to see that they were safe once or twice during the journey, and call for them as soon as they reached London, she'd have no trouble – 'please remember the porter, ma'am!' However, all was happily settled at last, and without any serious inconveniences they found themselves established in a first-class carriage, and presently after running smoothly at full speed across the rich English Midlands toward London and the eastern coast.

The extreme greenness of the October landscape was what struck them at first, and the wonderfully orderly and trim aspect of the country, with no ragged, stump-dotted fields or reaches of wild untended woods. Late in October as it was, the hedgerows and meadows were still almost summer-like in colour, though the trees were leafless. The delightful old manor houses and farm-houses of which they had glimpses now and again, were a constant pleasure to Katy, with their mullioned windows, twisted chimney stacks, porches of quaint build, and thick-growing ivy. She contrasted them with the uncompromising ugliness of farmhouses she remembered at home, and wondered whether it could be that at the end of another thousand years or so America would have picturesque buildings like those to show in addition to her picturesque scenery.

Suddenly, into the midst of these reflections there glanced a picture so vivid that it almost took away her breath, as the train steamed past a pack of hounds in full cry, followed by a galloping throng of scarlet-coated huntsmen. One horse and rider were in the air, going over a wall. Another was just rising to the leap. A string of others, headed by a lady, were tearing across a meadow bounded by a little brook, and beyond that streamed the hounds following the invisible fox. It was like one of Muybridge's instantaneous photographs of 'The Horse in Motion', for the moment that it lasted, and Katy put it away in her memory, distinct and brilliant, as she might a real picture.

Their destination in London was Batt's Hotel in Dover Street. The old gentleman on the *Spartacus*, who had 'crossed' so many times, had furnished Mrs Ashe with a number of addresses of hotels and lodging houses, from among which Katy had chosen Batt's for the reason that it was mentioned in Miss Edgeworth's *Patronage*. 'It was the place,' she explained, 'where Godfrey Percy didn't stay when Lord Oldborough sent him the letter.' It seemed an odd enough reason for going anywhere, that a person in a novel didn't stay there. But Mrs Ashe knew nothing of London, and had no preference of her own, so she was perfectly willing to give Katy hers; and Batt's was decided upon.

'It is just like a dream or a story,' said Katy, as they drove away from the London station in a four-wheeler. 'It is really ourselves, and this is really London. Can you imagine it?'

She looked out. Nothing met her eyes but dingy weather, muddy streets, long rows of ordinary brick or stone houses. It might very well have been New York or Boston on a foggy day, yet to her eyes all things had a subtle difference which made them unlike similar objects at home.

'Wimpole Street!' she cried suddenly, as she caught sight of the name on the corner, 'that is the street where Maria Crawford in *Mansfield Park*, you know, "opened one of the best houses" after she married Mr Rushworth. Think of seeing Wimpole Street! What fun!' She looked eagerly out after the 'best houses', but the whole street looked uninteresting and old fashioned; the best house to be seen was not of a kind, Katy thought, to reconcile an ambitious young woman to a dull husband. Katy had to remind herself that Miss Austen wrote her novels nearly a century ago, that London was a 'growing' place, and that things were probably much changed since that day.

More 'fun' awaited them when they arrived at Batt's, and exactly such a landlady sailed forth to welcome them as they had often met with in books – an old landlady, smiling and rubicund, with a towering lace cap on her head, a flowered silk gown, a gold chain, and a pair of fat mittened hands demurely crossed over a black brocade apron. She alone would have been worth crossing the ocean to see, they all declared. Their telegram had been received, and rooms were ready, with a bright, smoky fire of soft coals; the dinner table was set, and a nice, formal, white-cravatted old waiter, who seemed to have stepped out of the same book with the landlady, was waiting to serve it. Everything was dingy and old fashioned, but very clean and comfortable, and Katy concluded that on the whole Godfrey Percy would have done wisely to go to Batt's, and could have fared no better at the other hotel where he did stay.

The first of Katy's 'London sights' came to her next morning before she was out of her bedroom. She heard a bell ring and a queer, squeaking little voice utter a speech of which she could not make out a single world. Then came a laugh and a shout, as if several boys were amused at something or other; altogether her curiosity was roused, so that she finished dressing as fast as she could, and ran to the drawing room window, which commanded a view of the street. Quite a little crowd was collected under the window, and in their midst was a queer box raised high on poles, with little red curtains tied back on either side to form a miniature stage, on which puppets were moving and vociferating. Katy knew in a moment that she was seeing her first Punch and Judy show!

The box and the crowd began to move away. Katy, in despair, ran to Wilkins, the old waiter, who was setting the breakfast table.

'Oh, please stop that man!' she said. 'I want to see him.'

'What man is it, miss?' said Wilkins.

When he reached the window, and realized what Katy meant, his sense of propriety seemed to receive a severe shock. He even ventured on remonstrance.

'H'I wouldn't, miss, h'if h'I was you. Them Punches are a low lot, miss; they h'ought to be put down, really they h'ought. Gentlefolks, h'as a general thing, pays no h'attention to them.'

But Katy didn't care what 'gentlefolk' did or did not do, and insisted upon having Punch called back. So Wilkins was forced to swallow his remonstrances and his dignity, and go in pursuit of the objectionable object. Amy came rushing out, with her hair flying, and Mabel in her arms, and she and Katy had a real treat of Punch and Judy, with all the well-known scenes, and perhaps a few new ones thrown in for their especial pleasure; for the showman seemed to be inspired by the rapturous enjoyment of his little audience of three at the first-floor windows. Punch beat Judy and stole the baby, and Judy banged Punch in return, and the constable came in, and Punch outwitted him, and the hangman and the devil made their appearance duly; it was all perfectly satisfactory, and 'just exactly what she hoped it would be, and it quite made up for the muffins', Katy declared.

Then, when Punch had gone away, the question arose as to what they should choose out of the many delightful things in London, for their first morning.

Like ninety-nine Americans out of a hundred, they decided on Westminster Abbey, and indeed there is nothing in England more worthy of being seen or more impressive, in its dim, rich antiquity, to eyes fresh from the world which still calls itself 'new'. So to the Abbey they went, and lingered there till Mrs Ashe declared herself to be absolutely dropping with fatigue.

'If you don't take me home and give me something to eat,' she said, 'I shall drop down on one of these pedestals and stay there and be exhibited for ever after as an "h'effigy" of somebody belonging to ancient English history.'

So Katy tore herself away from Henry the Seventh and the Poet's Corner, and tore Amy away from a quaint little tomb shaped like a cradle, with the marble image of a baby in it, which had greatly taken the child's fancy. Amy could only be consoled by the promise that she should soon come again and stay as long as she liked.

She reminded Katy of this promise the very next morning.

'Mamma has waked up with rather a bad headache, and she thinks she will lie still and not come to breakfast,' she reported. 'And she sends her love, and says will you

please have a cab and go where you like, and if I won't be
a trouble, she would be glad if you would take me with
you. And I won't be a trouble, Miss Katy, and I know
where I wish you would go.'

'Where is that?'

'To see that cunning little baby again that we saw
yesterday. I want to show her to Mabel – she didn't go
with us, you know, and I don't like to have her mind not
improved; and, darling Miss Katy, mayn't I buy some
flowers and put them on the baby? She's so dusty and so
old that I don't believe anybody has put any flowers on
her for ever so long.'

Katy found this idea rather pretty, and willingly
stopped at Covent Garden, where they bought a bunch
of late roses for eighteen pence, which entirely satisfied
Amy. With them in her hand, and Mabel in her arms, she
led the way through the dim aisles of the Abbey, through
grates and doors, and up and down steps, the guide
following, but not at all needed, for Amy seemed to have
a perfectly clear recollection of every turn and winding.
When the chapel was reached, she laid the roses on the
tomb with gentle fingers, and a pitiful, reverent look in
her grey eyes. Then she lifted Mabel up to kiss the odd
little baby effigy above the marble quilt, whereupon the
guide seemed altogether surprised out of his composure,
and remarked to Katy:

'Little miss is an h'American, as is plain to see; no
h'English child would be likely to think of doing such a
thing.'

'Do not English children take any interest in the tombs
of the Abbey?' asked Katy.

'Oh, yes, m'm – h'interest; but they don't take no
special notice of one tomb above h'another.'

Katy could scarcely keep from laughing, especially as she heard Amy, who had been listening to the conversation, give an audible sniff, and inform Mabel that she was glad *she* was not an English child who didn't notice things, and liked grown-up graves as much as she did dear little cunning ones like this!

Later in the day, when Mrs Ashe was better, they all drove together to the quaint old keep which has been the scene of so many tragedies, and is known as the Tower of London. Here they were shown various rooms and chapels and prisons, including the apartments where Queen Elizabeth, when a friendless young princess, was shut up for many months by her sister, Queen Mary. Katy had read somewhere, and now told Amy, the pretty legend of the four little children who lived with their parents in the Tower, and used to play with the royal captive; and how one little boy brought her a key which he had picked up on the ground, and said, 'Now you can go out when you will, lady'; and how the Lords of the Council, getting wind of it, sent for the children to question them, and frightened them and their friends almost to death, and forbade them to go near the princess again.

A story about children always brings the past much nearer to a child, and Amy's imagination was so excited by this tale that when they got to the darksome closet which is said to have been the prison of Sir Walter Raleigh, she marched out of it with a pale and wrathful face.

'If this is English history, I never mean to learn any more of it, and neither shall Mabel,' she declared.

But it is not possible for Amy or anyone else not to learn a great deal of history simply by going about London. So many places are associated with people or events, and seeing the places makes one care so much more for the people or the events that one insensibly questions and wonders. Katy, who had 'browsed' all through her childhood in a good old-fashioned library, had her memory stuffed with all manner of little scraps of information and literary allusions, which now came into use. It was like owning the disjointed bits of a puzzle, and suddenly discovering that properly put together they make a pattern. Mrs Ashe, who had never been much of a reader, considered her young friend a prodigy of intelligence; but Katy herself realized how inadequate and inexact her knowledge was, and how many bits were missing from the pattern of her puzzle. She wished with all her heart, as everyone wishes under such circumstances, that she had studied harder and more wisely while the chance was in her power. On a journey you cannot read to advantage. Remember that, dear girls, who are looking forward to travelling some day, and be industrious in time.

October is not a favourable month in which to see England. Water, water is everywhere; you breathe it; you absorb it; it wets your clothes and it dampens your spirits. Mrs Ashe's friends advised her not to think of Scotland at that time of the year. One by one their little intended excursions were given up. A single day and night in Oxford and Stratford-on-Avon; a short visit to the Isle of Wight, where, in a country place which seemed provokingly pretty as far as they could see it for the rain, lived that friend of Mrs Ashe who had married an Englishman, and in so doing had, as Katy privately thought, 'renounced the sun'; a peep at Stonehenge from under the shelter of an umbrella, and an hour or two in

Salisbury Cathedral – this was all that they accomplished, except a brief halt at Winchester, that Katy might have the privilege of seeing the grave of her beloved Miss Austen. Katy had come abroad with a terribly long list of graves to visit, Mrs Ashe declared. They laid a few rainwashed flowers upon the tomb, and listened with edification to the verger, who inquired:

'Whatever was it, ma'am, that lady did which brings so many h'Americans to h'ask about her? Our h'English people don't seem to take the same h'interest.'

'She wrote such delightful stories,' explained Katy, but the old verger shook his head.

'I think h'it must be some other party, miss, you've confused with this here. It stands to reason, miss, that we'd have heard of 'em h'over 'ere in England sooner than you would h'over there in h'America, if the books 'ad been h'anything so h'extraordinary.'

The night after their return to London they were dining for the second time with the cousins of whom Mrs Ashe had spoken to Dr Carr, and as it happened Katy sat next to a quaint elderly American, who had lived for twenty years in London and knew it much better than most Londoners do. This gentleman, Mr Allen Beach, had a hobby for antiquities, old books especially, and passed half his time at the British Museum, and the other half in sale-rooms and the old shops in Wardour Street.

Katy was lamenting over the bad weather which stood in the way of their plans.

'It is so vexatious!' she said. 'Mrs Ashe meant to go to York and Lincoln and all the cathedral towns and to Scotland, and we have had to give it all up because of the rain. We shall go away having seen hardly anything.'

'You can see London.'

'We have – that is, we have seen the things that everybody sees.'

'But there are so many things that people in general do not see. How much longer are you to stay, Miss Carr?'

'A week, I believe.'

'Why don't you make out a list of old buildings which are connected with famous people in history, and visit them in turn? I did that the second year after I came. I gave up three months to it, and it was most interesting. I unearthed all manner of curious stories and traditions.'

'Or,' cried Katy, struck with a sudden bright thought, 'why mightn't I put into the list some of the places I know about in books – novels as well as history – and the places where the people who wrote the books lived?'

'You might do that, and it wouldn't be a bad idea, either,' said Mr Beach, pleased with her enthusiasm. 'I will get a pencil after dinner, and help you with your list if you will allow me.'

Mr Beach was better than his word. He not only suggested places and traced a plan of sightseeing, but on two different mornings he went with them himself; his intelligent knowledge of London added very much to the interest of the excursions. Under his guidance the little party of four – Mabel was never left out for it was *such* a chance for her to improve her mind, Amy declared – visited the Charterhouse, where Thackeray went to school, and the Home of the Poor Brothers connected with it, in which Colonel Newcome answered 'Adsum' to the roll call of the angels. They took a look at the small house in Curzon Street, which is supposed to have been in Thackeray's mind when he described the residence of Becky Sharp, and the other house in Russell Square which is unmistakably that where George Osborne courted Amelia Sedley. They went to service in the delightful old church of St Mary in the Temple, and thought of Ivanhoe and Brian de Bois-Guilbert and Rebecca the Jewess. From there Mr Beach took them to Lamb's Court, where Pendennis and George Warrington dwelt in chambers together; and to Brick Court, where Oliver Goldsmith passed so much of his life; and to the little rooms in which Charles and Mary Lamb spent so many sadly happy years. On another day they drove to Whitefriars, for the sake of Lord Glenvarloch and the old privilege of sanctuary in the *Fortunes of Nigel*; they took a peep at Bethnal Green, where the Blind Beggar and his 'Pretty Bessee' lived; and at the old prison of the Marshalsea, made interesting by its associations with *Little Dorrit*. They also went to see Milton's house and St Giles Church, in which he is buried, and stood a long time before St James's Palace, trying to make out which could have been Miss Burney's windows when she was dresser to Queen Charlotte. They saw Paternoster Row, and No. 5 Cheyne Walk, sacred forever to the memory of Thomas Carlyle, and Whitehall, where Queen Elizabeth lay in state and King Charles was beheaded, and the state rooms of Holland House; and by great good luck had a glimpse of George Eliot getting out of a cab. She stood for a moment while she gave her fare to the cabman, and Katy looked as one who might not look again, and carried away a distinct picture of the unbeautiful, interesting, remarkable face.

With all this to see and to do, the last week sped all too swiftly, and the last day came before they were at all ready to leave what Katy called 'story-book England'. Mrs Ashe had decided to cross by Newhaven and Dieppe, because someone had told her of the beautiful old town of Rouen, and it seemed easy and convenient to take it on the way to Paris. Having just landed from the long voyage across the Atlantic, the little passage of the Channel seemed nothing to our travellers, and they made ready for their night on the Dieppe steamer, with the philosophy which is born of ignorance. They were speedily undeceived!

The English Channel has a character of its own, which distinguishes it from other seas and straits. It seems made fractious and difficult by nature, and set as on purpose to be barrier between two nations who are too unlike to easily understand each other, and are the safer neighbours for this wholesome difficulty of communication between them. The 'chop' was worse than usual on the night when our travellers crossed; the steamer had to fight her way inch by inch. And oh, such a little steamer! And oh, such a long night!

CHAPTER
6
ACROSS THE CHANNEL

Dawn had given place to day, and day was well advanced toward noon, before the stout little steamer gained her port. It was hours after the usual time for arrival; the train for Paris must long since have started, and Katy felt dejected and forlorn as, making her way out of the terrible ladies' cabin, she crept on deck for her first glimpse of France.

The sun was struggling through the fog with a watery smile, and his faint beams shone on a confusion of stone piers, higher than the vessel's deck, intersected with canal-like waterways, through whose intricate windings the steamer was slowly threading her course to the landing place. Looking up, Katy could see crowds of people assembled to watch the boat come in – workmen, peasants, women, children, soldiers, custom-house officers, moving to and fro – and all this crowd were talking all at once and all were talking French.

I don't know why this should have startled her as it did. She knew, of course, that people of different countries were liable to be found speaking their own languages, but somehow the spectacle of the chattering multitude, all seeming so perfectly at ease with their preterites and subjunctives and never once having to refer to Ollendorf or a dictionary, filled her with a sense of dismayed surprise.

'Good gracious!' she said to herself, 'even the babies understand it!' She racked her brains to recall what she had once known of French, but very little seemed to have survived the horrors of the night!

'Oh, dear! what is the word for trunk key?' she asked herself. 'They will all begin to ask questions, and I shall not have a word to say, and Mrs Ashe will be even worse off, I know.' She saw the red-trousered custom-house officers pounce upon the passengers as they landed one by one, and she felt her heart sink within her.

But after all, when the time came, it did not prove so very bad. Katy's pleasant looks and courteous manner stood her in good stead. She did not trust herself to say much, but the officials seemed to understand without saying. They bowed and gestured, whisked the keys in and out, and in a surprisingly short time all was pronounced right – the baggage had 'passed', and it and its owners were free to proceed to the railway station, which fortunately was close at hand.

Inquiry revealed the fact that no train for Paris left till four in the afternoon.

'I am rather glad,' declared poor Mrs Ashe, 'for I feel too used up to move. I will lie here on this sofa, and, Katy dear, please see if there is an eating place, and get some breakfast for yourself and Amy, and send me a cup of tea.'

'I don't like to leave you alone,' Katy was beginning, but at that moment a nice old woman, who seemed to be in charge of the waiting room, appeared, and with a flood of French which none of them could follow, but which was evidently sympathetic in its nature, flew at Mrs Ashe and began to make her comfortable. From a cupboard in the wall she produced a pillow, from another cupboard a blanket; in a trice she had one under Mrs Ashe's head and the other wrapped round her feet.

'*Pauvre madame,*' she said, '*si pâle! Si souffrante! Il faut avoir quelque chose à boire et à manger tout de suite.*' She trotted across the room and into the restaurant which opened out of it, while Mrs Ashe smiled at Katy and said, 'You see, you can leave me quite safely; I am to be taken care of.' And Katy and Amy passed through the same door into the *buffet*, and sat down at a little table.

It was a particularly pleasant-looking place to breakfast in. There were many windows with bright polished panes and very clean short muslin curtains, and on the window sills stood rows of thrifty potted plants in full bloom – marigolds, balsams, nasturtiums, and many-coloured geraniums. Two birds in cages were singing loudly; the floor was waxed to a glass-like polish; nothing could have been whiter than the marble of the tables except the napkins laid over them. And such a good breakfast as was presently brought to them – delicious coffee in bowl-like cups, crisp rolls and rusks, an omelette with a delicate flavour of fine herbs, stewed chicken, little pats of freshly churned butter without salt, shaped like shells and tasting like solidified cream, and a pot of some sort of nice preserve. Amy made great delightful eyes at Katy, and remarking, 'I think France is heaps nicer than that old England,' began to eat with a will; and Katy herself felt that if this railroad meal was a specimen of what they had to expect in the future, they had indeed come to a land of plenty.

Fortified with the satisfactory breakfast, she felt equal to a walk, and after they had made sure that Mrs Ashe had all she needed, she and Amy (and Mabel) set off by themselves to see the sights of Dieppe. I don't know that travellers generally have considered Dieppe an interesting place, but Katy found it so. There was a really old church and some quaint buildings of the style of two centuries back, and even the more modern streets had a novel look to her unaccustomed eyes. At first they only ventured a timid turn or two, marking each corner, and going back now and then to reassure themselves by a look at the station; but after a while, growing bolder, Katy ventured to ask a question or two in French, and was surprised and charmed to find herself understood. After that she grew adventurous, and, no longer fearful of being lost, led Amy straight down a long street lined with shops, almost all of which were for the sale of various articles in ivory.

Ivory wares are one of the chief industries of Dieppe. There were cases full, windows full, and counters full, of the most exquisite combs and brushes, some with elaborate monograms in silver and colours, and others plain; there were boxes and caskets of every size and shape, ornaments, fans, parasol handles, looking glasses, frames for pictures large and small, and napkin rings.

Katy was particularly smitten with a paper knife in the form of an angel, with long, slender wings raised over its head and meeting to form a point. Its price was twenty francs, and she was strongly tempted to buy it for Clover or Rose Red. But she said to herself sensibly: 'This is the first shop I have been into and the first thing I have really wanted to buy, and very likely as we go on I shall see things I like better and want more, so it would be foolish to do it. No, I won't.' And she resolutely turned her back on their ivory angel, and walked away.

The next turn brought them to a gay-looking little market place, where old women in white caps were sitting on the ground beside baskets and panniers full of apples, pears, and various queer and curly vegetables, none of which Katy recognized as familiar; fish of all shapes and colours were flapping in shallow tubs of sea water; there were piles of stockings, muffetees and comforters in vivid blue and red worsted, and coarse pottery glazed in bright patterns. The faces of the women were brown and wrinkled; there were no pretty ones among them, but their black eyes were full of life and quickness, and their fingers one and all clicked with knitting needles, as their tongues flew equally fast in the chatter and the chaffer, which went on without stop or stay, though customers did not seem to be many and sales were few.

Returning to the station they found that Mrs Ashe had been asleep during their absence, and seemed so much better that it was with greatly amended spirits that they took their places in the late afternoon train which was to set them down at Rouen. Katy said they were like the Wise Men of the East, 'following a star', in their choice of a hotel; for, having no better advice, they had decided upon one of those thus distinguished in Baedeker's Guide Book.

The star did not betray their confidence, for the Hôtel de la Cloche, to which it led them, proved to be quaint and old, and very pleasant of aspect. The lofty chambers, with their dimly frescoed ceilings, and beds curtained with faded patch, might to all appearances have been furnished about the time when 'Columbus crossed the ocean blue'; but everything was clean, and had an air of old-time respectability. The dining room, which was evidently of more modern build, opened into a square courtyard, where oleanders and lemon trees in boxes stood round the basin of a little fountain, whose tinkle and plash blended agreeably with the rattle of the knives and forks. In one corner of the room was a raised and railed platform, where, behind a desk, sat the mistress of the house, busy with her account books, but keeping an eye the while on all that went forward.

Mrs Ashe walked past this personage without taking any notice of her, as Americans are wont to do under such circumstances, but presently the observant Katy noticed that everyone else, as they went in or out of the room, addressed a bow or a civil remark to this lady. She quite blushed at the recollection afterward, as she made ready for bed.

'How rude we must have seemed!' she thought. 'I am afraid the people here think that Americans have *awful* manners, everybody is so polite. They said "*Bon soir*", and "*Merci*", and "*Voulez-vous avoir la bonté*" to the waiters even! Well, there is one thing – I am going to reform. Tomorrow I will be as polite as anybody. They will think that I am miraculously improved by one night on French soil, but, never mind! I am going to do it.'

She kept her resolution, and astonished Mrs Ashe next morning, by bowing to the dame on the platform in the most winning manner, and saying, '*Bon jour, madame,*' as they went by.

'But, Katy, who is that person? Why do you speak to her?'

'Don't you see that they all do? She is the landlady, I think; at all events, everybody bows to her. And just notice how prettily these ladies at the next table speak to the waiter. They do not order him to do things as we do at home. I noticed it last night, and I liked it so much that I made a resolution to get up and be as polite as the French themselves this morning.'

So all the time that they went about the sumptuous old city, rich in carvings and sculptures and traditions, while they were looking at the Cathedral and the wonderful church of St Ouen, and the Palace of Justice, and the 'Place of the Maid', where poor Jeanne d'Arc was burned and her ashes scattered to the winds, Katy remembered her manners, and smiled and bowed, and used courteous prefixes in a soft, pleasant voice; and as Mrs Ashe and Amy fell in with her example more or less, I think the guides and coachmen and the old women who showed them over the buildings felt that the air of France was very civilizing indeed, and that these strangers from savage countries over the sea were in a fair way to be as well bred as if they had been born in a more favoured part of the world!

Paris looked very modern after the peculiar quaint richness and air of the Middle Ages which distinguish Rouen. Rooms had been engaged for Mrs Ashe's party in a *pension* near the Arc de l'Étoile, and there they drove immediately on arriving. The rooms were not in the *pension* itself, but in a house close by – a sitting room with six mirrors, three clocks, and a pinched little grate about a foot wide, a dining room just large enough for a table and four chairs, and two bedrooms. A maid called Amandine had been detailed to take charge of these rooms and serve their meals.

Dampness, as Katy afterwards wrote to Clover, was the first impression they received of 'gay Paris'. The tiny fire in the tiny grate had only just been lighted, and the walls and the sheets and even the blankets felt chilly and moist to the touch. They spent their first evening in hanging the bedclothes round the grate and piling on fuel; they even set the mattresses up on edge to warm and dry! It was not very enlivening, it must be confessed. Amy had taken a cold, Mrs Ashe looked worried, and Katy thought of Burnet and the safety and comfort of home with a throb of longing.

The days that ensued were not brilliant enough to remove this impression. The November fogs seemed to have followed them across the Channel, and Paris remained enveloped in a wet blanket which dimmed and hid its usually brilliant features. Going about in cabs with the windows drawn up, and now and then making a rush through the wet into shops, was not exactly delightful, but it seemed pretty much all that they could do. It was worse for Amy, whose cold kept her indoors and denied her even the relaxation of the cab. Mrs Ashe had engaged a well-recommended elderly English maid to come every morning and take care of Amy while they were out; and with this respectable functionary, whose ideas were of a rigidly British type, and who did not speak a word of any language but her own, poor Amy was compelled to spend most of her time. Her only consolation was in persuading this serene attendant to take a part in the French lessons which she made a daily point of giving to Mabel out of her own little phrase book.

'Wilkins is getting on, I think,' she told Katy one night. 'She says "*Biscuit glacé*" quite nicely now. But I never will let her look at the book, though she always wants to, for if once she saw how the words are spelled, she would never in the world pronounce them right again. They look so very different, you know.'

Katy looked at Amy's pale little face and eager eyes with a real heartache. Her rapture when, at the end of the long dull afternoons, her mother returned to her, was touching. Paris was very *triste* to poor Amy, with all her happy facility for amusing herself, and Katy felt that the sooner they got away from it the better it would be. So, in spite of the delight which her brief glimpses at the Louvre gave her, and the fun it was to go about with Mrs Ashe and see her buy pretty things, and the real satisfaction she took in the one perfectly made walking suit to which she had treated herself, she was glad when the final day came, when the belated dressmakers and artistes in jackets and wraps had sent home their last wares, and the trunks were packed. It had been rather the fault of circumstances than of Paris, but Katy had not learned to love the beautiful capital as most Americans do, and did not feel at all as if she wanted her 'reward of virtue' to be to go there when she died! There must be more interesting places for live people, and ghosts too, to be found on the map of Europe, she was sure.

Next morning, as they drove slowly down the Champs-Élysées, and looked back for a last glimpse of the famous Arc, a bright object met their eyes, moving vaguely against the mist. It was the gay red wagon of the Bon Marché, carrying bundles home to the dwellers of some up-town street.

Katy burst out laughing. 'It is an emblem of Paris,' she said – 'of our Paris, I mean. It has been all Bon Marché and fog!'

'Miss Katy,' interrupted Amy, '*do* you like Europe? For

my part, I was never so disgusted with any place in my life!'

'Poor little bird, her views of "Europe" are rather dark just now, and no wonder,' said her mother. 'Never mind, darling, you shall have something pleasanter by and by if I can find it for you.'

'Burnet is a great deal pleasanter than Paris,' pronounced Amy, decidedly. 'It doesn't always keep raining there, and I can take walks, and I understand everything that people say.'

All that day they sped southward, and with every hour came a change in the aspect of their surroundings.

Now they made brief stops in large busy towns which seemed humming with industry. Now they whirled through grape countries with miles of vineyards, where the brown leaves still hung on the vines. Then again came glimpses of old Roman ruins, amphitheatres, viaducts, fragments of wall or arch; or a sudden chill betokened their approach to mountains, where snowy peaks could be seen on the far horizon. And when the long night ended and day roused them from broken slumbers, behold, the world was made over! Autumn had vanished, and the summer, which they thought fled for good, had taken his place. Green woods waved about them, fresh leaves were blowing in the wind, roses and hollyhocks beckoned from white-walled gardens; and before they had done with exclaiming and rejoicing, the Mediterranean shot into view, intensely blue, with white fringes of foam, white sails blowing across, white gulls flying above it, and over all a sky of the same exquisite blue, whose clouds were white as the drifting sails on the water below. They were at Marseilles.

It was like a glimpse of paradise to eyes fresh from

autumnal greys and glooms, as they sped along the lovely coast; every curve and turn showed new combinations of sea and shore, olive-crowned cliff and shining mountain peak. With every mile the blue became bluer, the wind softer, the feathery verdure more dense and summer-like. Hyères and Cannes and Antibes were passed, and then, as they rounded a long point, came the view of a sunshiny city lying on a sunlit shore; the train slackened its speed, and they knew that their journey's end was come and they were in Nice.

The place seemed to laugh with gaiety as they drove down the Promenade des Anglais and past the English garden, where the band was playing beneath the acacias and the palm trees. On one side was a line of bright-windowed hotels and *pensions*, with balconies and striped awnings; on the other, the long reach of yellow sandy beach, where ladies were grouped on shawls and rugs, and children ran up and down in the sun, while beyond stretched the waveless sea. The December sun felt as warm as on a late June day at home, and had the same soft caressing touch. The pavements were thronged with groups of leisurely-looking people, all wearing an unmistakable holiday aspect; pretty girls in correct Parisian costumes walked demurely beside their mothers, with cavaliers in attendance. And among these young men appeared now and again the well-known uniform of the United States Navy.

'I wonder,' said Mrs Ashe, struck by a sudden thought, 'if by any chance our squadron is here.' She asked the question the moment they entered the hotel, and the porter, who prided himself on understanding 'zose Eenglesh', replied:

'Mais oui, madame, ze Americaine fleet it is here; zat is,

not here, but at Villefranche, just a leetle four mile away – it is ze same zing exactly.'

'Katy, do you hear that?' cried Mrs Ashe. 'The frigates *are* here, and the *Natchitoches* among them of course; so we shall have Ned to go about with us everywhere. It is a real piece of good luck for us. Ladies are at such a loss in a place like this, with nobody to escort them. I am perfectly delighted.'

'So am I,' said Katy. 'I never saw a frigate, and I always wanted to see one. Do you suppose they will let us go on board?'

'Why, of course they will.' Then to the porter: 'Give me a sheet of paper and an envelope, please – I must let Ned know that I am here at once.'

Mrs Ashe wrote her note and despatched it before they went upstairs to take off their bonnets. She seemed to have half a hope that some bird of the air might carry the news of her arrival to her brother, for she kept running to the window as if in expectation of seeing him. She was too restless to lie down or sleep, and after she and Katy had lunched, proposed that they should go out on the beach for a while.

'Perhaps we may come across Ned,' she remarked.

They did not come across Ned, but there was no lack of other delightful objects to engage their attention. The sands were smooth and hard as a floor. Soft pink lights were beginning to tinge the western sky. To the north shone the peaks of the maritime Alps, and the same rosy glow caught them here and there, and warmed their greys and whites into colour.

'I wonder what that can be!' said Katy, indicating the rocky point which bounded the beach to the east, where stood a picturesque building of stone, with massive towers and steep pitches of roof. 'It looks half like a house and half like a castle, but it is quite fascinating, I think. Do you suppose that people live there?'

'We might ask,' suggested Mrs Ashe.

Just then they came to a shallow river spanned by a bridge, beside whose pebbly bed stood a number of women who seemed to be washing clothes by the simple and primitive process of laying them in the water on top of the stones, and pounding them with a flat wooden paddle till they were white. Katy privately thought that the clothes stood a poor chance of lasting through these cleansing operations, but she did not say so, and made the inquiry which Mrs Ashe had suggested, in her best French.

'*Celle-là?*' answered the old woman whom she had addressed. '*Mais c'est la Pension Suisse.*'

'A *pension!* Why, that means a boarding house!' cried Katy. 'What fun it must be to board there!'

'Well, why shouldn't we board there?' said her friend. 'You know we meant to look for rooms as soon as we were rested and had found out a little about the place. Let us walk on and see what the Pension Suisse is like. If the inside is as pleasant as the outside, we could not do better, I should think.'

'Oh, I do hope all the rooms are not already taken!' said Katy, who had fallen in love at first sight with the Pension Suisse. She felt quite oppressed with anxiety as they rang the bell.

The Pension Suisse proved to be quite as charming inside as out. The thick stone walls made deep sills and embrasures for the casement windows, which were furnished with red cushions to serve as seats and lounging places. Every window seemed to command a view, for those which did not look toward the sea looked toward the mountains. The house was by no means full either. Several sets of rooms were to be had, and Katy felt as if she had walked straight into the pages of a romance when Mrs Ashe engaged for a month a delightful suite of three, comprising a sitting room and two sleeping chambers, in a round tower, with a balcony overhanging the water. There was a side window, from which a flight of steps led down into a little walled garden, nestled in among the masonry, where tall laurustinus and lemon trees grew, and orange and brown wallflowers made the air sweet. Her contentment knew no bounds.

'I am so glad that I came!' she told Mrs Ashe. 'I never confessed it to you before, but sometimes – when we were sick at sea, you know, and when it would rain all the time, and after Amy caught that cold in Paris – I have almost wished, just for a minute or two at a time, that we hadn't. But now I wouldn't not have come for the world! This is perfectly delicious. I am glad, glad, glad we are here, and we are going to have a lovely time, I know.'

They were passing out of the rooms into the hall as she said these words, and two ladies who were walking up a cross passage turned their heads at the sound of her voice. To her great surprise Katy recognized Mrs Page and Lilly.

'Why, Cousin Olivia, is it you?' she cried, springing forward with the cordiality one naturally feels in seeing a familiar face in a foreign land.

Mrs Page seemed rather more puzzled than cordial. She put up her eyeglass and did not seem to quite make out who Katy was.

'It is Katy Carr, Mamma,' explained Lilly. 'Well, Katy,

this *is* a surprise! Who would have thought of meeting you in Nice?'

There was a decided absence of rapture in Lilly's manner. She was prettier than ever, as Katy saw in a moment, and beautifully dressed in soft brown velvet, which exactly suited her complexion and her pale-coloured wavy hair.

'Katy Carr! Why, so it is!' admitted Mrs Page. 'It is a surprise indeed. We had no idea that you were abroad. What has brought you so far from Tunket – Burnet, I mean? Who are you with?'

'With my friend Mrs Ashe,' explained Katy, rather chilled by this cool reception. 'Let me introduce you. Mrs Ashe, these are my cousins, Mrs Page and Miss Page. Amy – why, where is Amy?'

Amy had walked back to the door of the garden staircase, and was standing there looking down upon the flowers.

Cousin Olivia bowed rather distantly. Her quick eye took in the details of Mrs Ashe's travelling dress and Katy's dark-blue ulster.

'Some countrified friend from that dreadful Western town where they live,' she said to herself. 'How foolish of Philip Carr to try to send his girls to Europe! He can't afford it, I know.' Her voice was rather rigid as she inquired:

'And what brings you here – to this house, I mean?'

'Oh, we are coming tomorrow to stay! We have taken rooms for a month,' explained Katy. 'What a delicious-looking old place it is!'

'Have you?' said Lilly, in a voice which did not express any particular pleasure. 'Why, we are staying here too.'

CHAPTER
7

THE PENSION SUISSE

'What do you suppose can have brought Katy Carr to Europe?' inquired Lilly, as she stood in the window watching the three figures walk slowly down the sands. 'She is the last person I expected to turn up here. I supposed she was stuck in that horrid place – what is the name of it? – where they live, for the rest of her life.'

'I confess I am surprised at meeting her myself,' rejoined Mrs Page. 'I had no idea that her father could afford so expensive a journey.'

'And who is this woman that she has got along with her?'

'I have no idea, I'm sure. Some Western friend, I suppose.'

'Dear me! I wish they were going to some other house than this,' said Lilly discontentedly. 'If they were at the Rivoir, for instance, or one of those places at the far end of the beach, we shouldn't need to see anything of them, or even know that they were in town! It's a real nuisance to have people spring upon you this way, people you don't want to meet; and when they happen to be relations it is all the worse. Katy will be hanging on us all the time, I'm afraid.'

'Oh, my dear, there is no fear of that! A little repression on our part will prevent her from being any trouble, I'm quite certain. But we *must* treat her politely, you know, Lilly; her father is my cousin.'

'That's the saddest part of it! Well, there's one thing, I shall *not* take her with me every time we go to the frigates,' said Lilly decisively. 'I am not going to inflict a country cousin on Lieutenant Worthington, and spoil all my own fun beside. So I give you fair warning, Mamma, and you must manage it somehow.'

'Certainly, dear, I will. It would be a great pity to have your visit to Nice spoiled in any way, with the squadron here, too, and that pleasant Mr Worthington so very attentive.'

Unconscious of these plans for her suppression, Katy walked back to the hotel in a mood of pensive pleasure. Europe at last promised to be as delightful as it had seemed when she only knew it from maps and books, and Nice so far appeared to her the most charming place in the world.

Somebody was waiting for them at the Hôtel des Anglais – a tall, bronzed, good-looking somebody in uniform, with pleasant brown eyes beaming from beneath a gold-banded cap; at the sight of whom Amy rushed forward with her long locks flying, and Mrs Ashe uttered an exclamation of pleasure. It was Ned Worthington, Mrs Ashe's only brother, whom she had not met for two years and a half, and you can easily imagine how glad she was to see him.

'You got my note then?' she said, after the first eager greetings were over and she had introduced him to Katy.

'Note? No. Did you write me a note?'

'Yes; to Villefranche.'

'To the ship? I shan't get that till tomorrow. No; finding out that you were here is just a bit of good fortune. I came over to call on some friends who are staying down the beach a little way, and, dropping in to look over the list of arrivals, as I generally do, I saw your names; the porter not being able to say which way you had gone, I waited for you to come in.'

'We have been looking at such a delightful old place, the Pension Suisse, and have taken rooms.'

'The Pension Suisse, eh? Why, that was where I was going to call. I know some people who are staying there. It seems a pleasant house; I'm glad you are going there, Polly. It's first-rate luck that the ships happen to be here just now. I can see you every day.'

'But, Ned, surely you are not leaving me so soon? Surely you will stay and dine with us?' urged his sister, as he took up his cap.

'I wish I could, but I can't tonight, Polly. You see I had engaged to take some ladies out to drive, and they will expect me. I had no idea that you would be here, or I should have kept myself free,' he said apologetically. 'Tomorrow I will come over early, and be at your service for whatever you like to do.'

'That's right, dear boy. We shall expect you.' Then the moment he was gone: 'Now, Katy, isn't he nice?'

'Very nice, I should think,' said Katy, who had watched the brief interview with interest. 'I like his face so much, and how fond he is of you!'

'Dear fellow! So he is. I am seven years older than he, but we have always been intimate. Brothers and sisters are not always intimate, you know – or perhaps you don't know, for yours are.'

'Yes, indeed,' said Katy, with a happy smile. 'There is

nobody like Clover and Elsie, except perhaps Johnnie and Dorry and Phil,' she added, with a laugh.

The remove to the Pension Suisse was made early the next morning. Mrs Page and Lilly did not appear to welcome them. Katy rather rejoiced in their absence, for she wanted the chance to get into order without interruptions. There was something comfortable in the thought that they were to stay a whole month in these new quarters; for so long a time it seemed worth while to make them pretty and homelike. So, while Mrs Ashe unpacked her own belongings and Amy's, Katy, who had a natural turn for arranging rooms, took possession of the little parlour, pulled the furniture into new positions, laid out portfolios and work cases and their few books, pinned various photographs which they had bought in Oxford and London on the walls, and tied back the curtains to admit the sunshine. Then she paid a visit to the little garden, and came back with a long branch of laurustinus, which she trained across the mantelpiece, and a bunch of wallflowers for their one little vase. The maid, by her orders, laid a fire of wood and pine cones ready for lighting, and when all was done she called Mrs Ashe to pronounce upon the effect.

'It is lovely,' she said, sinking into a great velvet armchair which Katy had drawn close to the seaward window. 'I haven't seen anything so pleasant since we left home. You are a witch, Katy, and the comfort of my life. I am so glad I brought you! Now, pray go and unpack your own things, and make yourself look nice for the second breakfast. We have been a shabby set enough since we arrived. I saw those cousins of yours looking askance at our old travelling dresses yesterday. Let us try to make a more respectable impression today.'

So they went down to breakfast, Mrs Ashe in one of her new Paris gowns, Katy in a pretty dress of olive serge, and Amy all smiles and ruffled pinafore, walking hand in hand with her Uncle Ned, who had just arrived, and whose great ally she was. Mrs Page and Lilly, who were already seated at table, had much ado to conceal their somewhat unflattering surprise at the conjunction. For one moment Lilly's eyes opened into a wild stare of incredulous astonishment; then she remembered herself, nodded as pleasantly as she could to Mrs Ashe and Katy, and favoured Lieutenant Worthington with a pretty blushing smile as he went by, while she murmured:

'Mamma, do you see that? What does it mean?'

'Why, Ned, do you know those people?' asked Mrs Ashe at the same moment.

'Do *you* know them?'

'Yes, we met yesterday. They are connexions of my friend Miss Carr.'

'Really? There is not the least family likeness between them.' And Mr Worthington's eyes travelled deliberately from Lilly's delicate golden prettiness to Katy, who, truth to say, did not shine by the contrast.

'She has a nice, sensible sort of face,' he thought, 'and she looks like a lady, but for beauty there is no comparison between the two.' Then he turned to listen to his sister as she replied:

'No, indeed, not the least; no two girls could be less like.' Mrs Ashe had made the same comparison, but with quite a different result. Katy's face was grown dear to her, and she had not taken the smallest fancy to Lilly Page.

Her relationship to the young naval officer, however, made a wonderful difference in the attitude of Mrs Page and Lilly toward the party. Katy became a person to be cultivated rather than repressed, and thenceforward there was no lack of cordiality on their part.

'I want to come in and have a good talk,' said Lilly, slipping her arm through Katy's as they left the dining room. 'Mayn't I come now while mamma is calling on Mrs Ashe?' This arrangement brought her to the side of Lieutenant Worthington, and she walked between him and Katy down the hall and into the little drawing room.

'Oh, how perfectly charming! You have been fixing up ever since you came, haven't you? It looks like home. I wish we had a *salon*, but mamma thought it wasn't worth while, as we were only to be here such a little time. What a delicious balcony over the water, too! May I go out on it? Oh, Mr Worthington, do see this!'

She pushed open the half-closed window and stepped out as she spoke. Mr Worthington, after hesitating a moment, followed. Katy paused uncertain. There was hardly room for three on the balcony, yet she did not quite like to leave them. But Lilly had turned her back, and was talking in a low tone; it was nothing more in reality than the lightest chit-chat, but it had the air of being something confidential, so Katy, after waiting a little while, retreated to the sofa and took up her work, joining now and then in the conversation which Mrs Ashe was keeping up with Cousin Olivia. She did not mind Lilly's ill breeding, nor was she surprised at it. Mrs Ashe was less tolerant.

'Isn't it rather damp out there, Ned?' she called to her brother; 'you had better throw my shawl round Miss Page's shoulders.'

'Oh, it isn't a bit damp!' said Lilly, recalled to herself by this broad hint. 'Thank you so much for thinking of it,

Mrs Ashe, but I am just coming in.' She seated herself beside Katy, and began to question her rather languidly.

'When did you leave home, and how were they all when you came away?'

'All well, thank you. We sailed from Boston on the fourteenth of October; before that I spent two days with Rose Red – you remember her? She is married now, and has the dearest little home and such a darling baby!'

'Yes, I heard of her marriage. It didn't seem much of a match for Mr Redding's daughter to make, did it? I never supposed she would be satisfied with anything less than a member of Congress or a Secretary of Legation.'

'Rose isn't particularly ambitious, I think, and she seems perfectly happy,' replied Katy flushing.

'Oh, you needn't fire up in her defence! You and Clover always did adore Rose Red, I know, but I never could see what there was about her that was so wonderfully fascinating. She never had the least style, and she was always just as rude to me as she could be.'

'You were not intimate at school, but I am sure Rose was never rude,' said Katy with spirit.

'Well, we won't fight about her at this late day. Tell me where you have been, and where you are going, and how long you are to stay in Europe.'

Katy, glad to change the subject, complied, and the conversation diverged into comparison of plans and experiences. Lilly had been in Europe nearly a year, and had seen 'almost everything', as she phrased it. She and her mother had spent the previous winter in Italy, had taken a run into Russia, 'done' Switzerland and the Tyrol thoroughly, and France and Germany, and were soon going into Spain, and from there to Paris, to shop, in preparation for their return home in the spring.

'Of course we shall want quantities of things,' she said. 'No one will believe that we have been abroad unless we bring home a lot of clothes. The *lingerie* and all that is ordered already, but the dresses must be made at the last moment, and we shall have a horrid time of it, I suppose. Worth has promised to make me two walking suits and two ball dresses, but he's very bad about keeping his word. Did you do much when you were in Paris, Katy?'

'We went to the Louvre three times, and to Versailles and St Cloud,' said Katy, wilfully misunderstanding her.

'Oh, I didn't mean that kind of stupid thing! I meant gowns. What did you buy?'

'One tailor-made suit of dark-blue cloth.'

'My! What moderation!'

Shopping played a large part in Lilly's reminiscences. She recollected places, not from their situation or beauty or historical associations, or because of the works of art which they contained, but as the places where she bought this or that.

'Oh, that dear Piazza di Spagna!' she would say, 'that was where I found my rococo necklace, the loveliest thing you ever saw, Katy.' Or, 'Prague – oh yes! Mother got the most enchanting old silver chatelaine there, with all kinds of things hanging on it – needle-cases and watches and scent bottles, all solid, and so beautifully chased.' Or again, 'Berlin was horrid, we thought; but the amber is better and cheaper than anywhere else – great strings of beads, of the largest size and that beautiful pale yellow, for a hundred francs. You must get yourself one, Katy.'

Poor Lilly! Europe to her was all 'things'. She had collected trunks full of objects to carry home, but of the other collections, which do not go into trunks, she had little or none. Her mind was as empty, her heart as untouched as ever; the beauty and the glory and the pathos of art and history and nature had been poured out in vain before her closed and indifferent eyes.

Life soon dropped into a peaceful routine at the Pension Suisse, which was at the same time restful and stimulating. Katy's first act in the morning, as soon as she opened her eyes, was to hurry to the window in hopes of getting a glimpse of Corsica. She had discovered that this elusive island could almost always be seen from Nice at the dawning, but that as soon as the sun was fairly up, it vanished, to appear no more for the rest of the day. There was something fascinating to her imagination in the hovering mountain outline between sea and sky. She felt as if she were under an engagement to be there to meet it, and she rarely missed the appointment. Then, after Corsica had pulled the bright mists over its face and melted from view, she would hurry with her dressing, and as soon as was practicable set to work to make the *salon* look bright before the coffee and rolls should appear, a little after eight o'clock. Mrs Ashe always found the fire lit, the little meal cosily set out beside it, and Katy's happy untroubled face to welcome her when she emerged from her room, and the cheer of these morning repasts made a good beginning for the day.

Then came walking and a French lesson, and a long sitting on the beach, while Katy worked at her home letters and Amy raced up and down in the sun; and then toward noon Lieutenant Ned generally appeared, and some scheme of pleasure was set on foot. Mrs Ashe ignored his evident *penchant* for Lilly Page and claimed his time and attentions as hers by right. Young Worthington was a good deal 'taken' with the pretty

Lilly; still, he had an old-time devotion for his sister and the habit of doing what she desired, and he yielded to her behests with no audible objections. He made a fourth in the carriage while they drove over the lovely hills which encircle Nice toward the north, to Cimiers and the Val de St André, or down the coast toward Ventimiglia. He went with them to Monte Carlo and Mentone, and was their escort again and again when they visited the great warships as they lay at anchor in a bay which in its translucent blue was like an enormous sapphire.

Mrs Page and her daughter were included in these parties more than once, but there was something in Mrs Ashe's cool appropriation of her brother which was infinitely vexatious to Lilly, who before her arrival had rather looked upon Lieutenant Worthington as her own especial property.

'I wish Mrs Ashe had stayed at home,' she told her mother. 'She quite spoils everything. Mr Worthington isn't half so nice as he was before she came. I do believe she has a plan for making him fall in love with Katy; but there she makes a miss of it, for he doesn't seem to care anything about her.'

'Katy is a girl nice enough,' pronounced her mother, 'but not the sort to attract a gay young man, I should fancy. I don't believe *she* is thinking of any such thing. You needn't be afraid, Lilly.'

'I'm not afraid,' said Lilly, with a pout, 'only it's so provoking!'

Mrs Page was quite right. Katy was not thinking of any such thing. She liked Ned Worthington's frank manners; she owned, quite honestly, that she thought him handsome, and she particularly admired the sort of deferential affection which he showed to Mrs Ashe, and his nice ways with Amy. For herself, she was aware that he scarcely noticed her except as politeness demanded that he should be civil to his sister's friend, but the knowledge did not trouble her particularly. Her head was full of interesting things, plans, ideas. She was not accustomed to being made the object of admiration, and experienced none of the vexations of a neglected belle. If Lieutenant Worthington happened to talk to her, she responded frankly and freely; if he did not, she occupied herself with something else. In either case she was quite unembarrassed both in feeling and manner, and had none of the awkwardness which comes from disappointed vanity and baffled expectations, and the need for concealing them.

Toward the close of December the officers of the flagship gave a ball, which was the great event of the season for the gay world of Nice. Americans were naturally in the ascendant on an American frigate, and of all the American girls present, Lilly Page was unquestionably the prettiest. Exquisitely dressed in white lace, with bands of turquoises on her neck and arms and in her hair, she had more partners than she knew what to do with, more bouquets than she could well carry, and compliments enough to turn any girl's head. Thrown off her guard by her triumphs, she indulged a little vindictive feeling which had been growing in her mind of late on account of what she chose to consider certain derelictions of duty on the part of Lieutenant Worthington, and treated him to a taste of neglect. She was engaged three deep when he asked her to dance; she did not hear when he invited her to walk; she turned a cold shoulder when he tried to talk, and seemed absorbed by the other cavaliers, naval and otherwise, who crowded about her.

Piqued and surprised, Ned Worthington turned to Katy. She did not dance, saying frankly that she did not know how, and was too tall; and she was rather simply dressed in a pearl-grey silk, which had been her best gown the winter before in Burnet, with a bunch of red roses in the white lace of the tucker, and another in her hand, both the gifts of little Amy; but she looked pleasant and serene, and there was something about her which somehow soothed his disturbed mind, as he offered her his arm for a walk on the decks.

For a while they said little, and Katy was quite content to pace up and down in silence, enjoying the really beautiful scene – the moonlight on the bay, the deep, wavering reflections of the dark hulls and slender spars, the fairy effect of the coloured lamps and lanterns, and the brilliant moving maze of the dancers.

'Do you care for this sort of thing?' he suddenly asked.

'What sort of thing do you mean?'

'Oh, all this jigging and waltzing and amusement!'

'I don't know how to "jig", but it's delightful to look on,' she answered merrily. 'I never saw anything so pretty in my life.'

The happy tone of her voice, and the unruffled face which she turned upon him, quieted his irritation.

'I really believe you mean it,' he said, 'and yet, if you won't think me rude to say so, most girls would consider the thing dull enough if they were only getting out of it what you are – if they were not dancing, I mean, and nobody in particular was trying to entertain them.'

'But everything *is* being done to entertain me,' cried Katy. 'I can't imagine what makes you think that it could seem dull. I am in it all, don't you see – I have my share – Oh, I am stupid, I can't make you understand!'

'Yes, you do. I understand perfectly, I think; only it is such a different point of view from what girls in general would take.' (By girls he meant Lilly!) 'Please do not think me uncivil.'

'You are not uncivil at all; but don't let us talk any more about me. Look at the lights between the shadows of the masts on the water. How they quiver! I never saw anything so beautiful, I think. And how warm it is! I can't believe that we are in December and that it is nearly Christmas.'

'How is Polly going to celebrate her Christmas? Have you decided?'

'Amy is to have a Christmas tree for her dolls, and two other dolls are coming. We went out this morning to buy things for it – tiny little toys and candles fit for Lilliput. And that reminds me, do you suppose one can get any Christmas greens here?'

'Why not? The place seems full of green.'

'That's just it; the summer look makes it unnatural. But I should like some to dress the parlour with, if they could be had.'

'I'll see what I can find, and send you a load.'

I don't know why this very simple little talk should have made an impression on Lieutenant Worthington's mind, but somehow he did not forget it.

'"Don't let us talk any more about me",' he said to himself, that night when alone in his cabin. 'I wonder how long it would be before the other one did anything to divert the talk from herself. Some time, I fancy.' He smiled rather grimly as he unbuckled his sword-belt. It is unlucky for a girl when she starts a train of reflection like this. Lilly's little attempt to pique her admirer had somehow missed its mark.

The next afternoon Katy, in her favourite place on the beach, was at work on the long weekly letter which she never failed to send home to Burnet. She held her portfolio in her lap, and her pen ran rapidly over the paper, as rapidly almost as her tongue would have run could her correspondents have been brought nearer.

Nice, 22 December

DEAR PAPA AND EVERYBODY,

Amy and I are sitting on my old purple cloak, which is spread over the sand just where it was spread the last time I wrote you. We are playing the following game: I am a fairy and she is a little girl. Another fairy – not sitting on the cloak at present – has enchanted the little girl, and I am telling her various ways by which she can work out her deliverance. At present the task is to find twenty-four dull red pebbles of the same colour, failing to do which she is to be changed into an owl. When we began to play, I was the wicked fairy, but Amy objected to that because I am 'so nice', so we changed the characters. I wish you could see the glee in her pretty grey eyes over this infantile game, into which she has thrown herself so thoroughly that she half believes in it. 'But I needn't really be changed into an owl!' she says, with a good deal of anxiety in her voice.

To think that you are shivering in the first snowstorm, or sending the children out with their sleds and india-rubbers to slide! How I wish instead that you were sharing the purple cloak with Amy and me, and could sit all this warm, balmy afternoon close to the surf-line which fringes this bluest of blue seas! There is plenty of room for you all. Not many people come down to this end of the beach, and if you were very good we would let you play.

Our life here goes on as delightfully as ever. Nice is very full of people, and there seem to be some pleasant ones among them. Here, at the Pension Suisse, we do not see a great many Americans. The fellow boarders are principally Germans and Austrians, with a sprinkling of French. (Amy has found her twenty-four red pebbles, so she is let off from being an owl. She is now engaged in throwing them one by one into the sea. Each must hit the water under penalty of her being turned into a muscovy duck. She doesn't know exactly what a muscovy duck is, which makes her all the more particular about her shots.) But, as I was saying, our little *suite* in the round tower is so on one side of the rest of the Pension that it is as good as having a house of our own. The *salon* is very bright and sunny; we have two sofas, and a square table, and a round table, and a sort of what-not, and two easy chairs, and two uneasy chairs, and a lamp of our own, and a clock. There is also a sofa-bed. There's richness for you! We have pinned up all our photographs on the walls, including Papa's and Clovy's, and that bad one of Phil and Johnnie making faces at each other, and three lovely red-and-yellow Japanese pictures on muslin which Rose Red put in my trunk the last thing, for a spot of colour. There are some autumn leaves too, and we always have flowers, and in the mornings and evenings a fire.

Amy is now finding fifty snow-white pebbles, which, when found, are to be interred in one common grave among the shingle. If she fails to do this, she is to be changed to an electric eel. The chief difficulty is that she loses her heart to particular pebbles. 'I can't bury you,' I hear her saying.

To return – we have jolly little breakfasts together in the *salon*. They consist of coffee and rolls, and are served by a droll, snappish little *garçon* with no teeth, and an Italian-French patois which is very hard to understand when he sputters. He told me the other day that he had been a *garçon* for forty-six years, which seemed rather a long boyhood.

The company, as we meet them at table, are rather entertaining. Cousin Olivia and Lilly are on their best behaviour to me because I am travelling with Mrs Ashe, and Mrs Ashe is Lieutenant Worthington's sister, and Lieutenant Worthington is Lilly's admirer, and they like him very much. In fact, Lilly has intimated confidentially that she is all but engaged to him, but I am not sure about it, or if that was what she meant; and I fear, if it proves true, that dear Polly will not like it at all. She is quite unmanageable, and snubs Lilly continually in a polite way, which makes me fidgety for fear Lilly will be offended, but she never seems to notice it. Cousin Olivia looks very handsome and gorgeous. She quite takes the colour out of the little Russian countess who sits next to her, and who is as dowdy and meek as if she came from Akron or Binghampton, or any other place where countesses are unknown. Then there are two charming, well-bred young Austrians. The one who sits nearest to me is a 'Candidat' for a Doctorate of Laws, and speaks eight languages well. He has only studied English for the past six weeks, but has made wonderful progress. I wish my French were half as good as his English is already.

There is a very gossiping young woman on the storey beneath ours, whom I meet sometimes in the garden, and from her I hear all manner of romantic tales about people in the house. One little French girl is dying of consumption and a broken heart, because of a quarrel with her lover, who is a courier; and the *padrona*, who is young and pretty, and has only been married a few months to our elderly landlord, has a story also. I forget some of the details, but there was a stern parent and an admirer, and a cup of cold poison, and now she says she wishes she were dying of consumption like poor Alphonsine. For all that, she looks quite fat and rosy, and I often see her in her best gown with a great deal of Roman scarf and mosaic jewellery, stationed in the doorway, 'making the Pension look attractive to the passers-by'. So she has a sense of duty, though she is unhappy.

Amy has buried all her pebbles, and says she is tired of playing fairy. She is now sitting with her head on my shoulder, and professedly studying her French verbs for tomorrow, but in reality, I am sorry to say, she is conversing with me about beheadings – a subject which, since her visit to the Tower, has exercised a horrible fascination over her mind. 'Do people die right away?' she asks. 'Don't they feel one minute, and doesn't it feel awfully?' There is a good deal of blood, she supposes, because there was so much straw laid about the block in the picture of Lady Jane Gray's execution, which enlivened our walls in Paris. On the whole, I am rather glad that a fat little white dog has come waddling down the beach and taken off her attention.

Speaking of Paris seems to renew the sense of fog which we had there. Oh, how enchanting sunshine is after weeks of gloom! I shall never forget how the Mediterranean looked when we saw it first – all blue, and such a lovely colour! There ought, according to Morse's Atlas, to have been a big red letter T on the water about where we were, but I didn't see any. Perhaps they letter it so far out from shore that only people in boats notice it.

Now the dusk is fading, and the odd chill which hides under these warm afternoons begins to be felt. Amy has received a message written on a mysterious white pebble to the effect –

Katy was interrupted at this point by a crunching step on the gravel behind her.

'Good afternoon!' said a voice. 'Polly has sent me to fetch you and Amy in. She says it is growing cool.'

'We were just coming,' said Katy, beginning to put away her papers.

Ned Worthington sat down on the cloak beside her. The distance was now steel grey against the sky; then came a stripe of violet, and then a broad sheet of the vivid iridescent blue which one sees on the necks of peacocks, which again melted into the long line of flashing surf.

'See that gull,' he said, 'how it drops plump into the sea, as if bound to go through to China!'

'Mrs Hawthorne calls skylarks "little raptures",' replied Katy. 'Seagulls seem to me like grown-up raptures.'

'Are you going?' said Lieutenant Worthington in a tone of surprise, as she rose.

'Didn't you say that Polly wanted us to come in?'

'Why, yes, but it seems too good to leave, doesn't it? Oh, by the way, Miss Carr, I came across a man today and ordered your greens! They will be sent on Christmas Eve. Is that right?'

'Quite right, and we are ever so much obliged to you.' She returned for a last look at the sea, and, unseen by Ned Worthington, formed her lips into a 'goodnight'. Katy had made great friends with the Mediterranean.

The promised greens appeared on the afternoon before Christmas Day, in the shape of an enormous faggot of laurel and laurustinus and holly and box, orange and lemon boughs with ripe fruit hanging from them, thick ivy tendrils whole yards long, arbutus, pepper tree, and great branches of acacia, covered with feathery yellow bloom. The man apologized for bringing so little. The gentleman had ordered two francs' worth, he said, but this was all he could carry; he would fetch some more if the young lady wished. But Katy, exclaiming with delight over her wealth, wished no more, so the man departed, and the three friends proceeded to turn the little *salon* into a fairy bower. Every photograph and picture was wreathed in ivy, long garlands hung on either side the windows, and the chimney piece and door frames became clustering banks of leaf and blossom. A great box of flowers had come with the greens, and bowls of fresh roses and heliotrope and carnations were set everywhere; violets and primroses, gold-hearted brown auriculas, spikes of veronica, all the zones and all the seasons combining to make Christmas-tide sweet, and to turn winter topsy-turvy in the little parlour.

Mabel and Maria Matilda, with their two doll visitors, sat gravely round the table, in the laps of their little mistresses, and Katy, putting on an apron and an improvised cap, and speaking Irish very fast, served them with a repast of rolls and cocoa, raspberry jam, and delicious

little almond cakes. The fun waxed fast and furious, and
Lieutenant Worthington, coming in with his hands full of
parcels for the Christmas tree, was just in time to hear
Katy remark in a strong County Kerry brogue:

'Och, thin indade, Miss Amy, and it's no more cake
you'll be getting out of me the night. That's four pieces
you've ate, and it's little shlape your poor mother'll git
with you a-tossin' and tumblin' forenenst her all night
long because of your big appetite.'

'Oh, Miss Katy, talk Irish some more!' cried the delighted children.

'Is it Irish you'd be afther having me talk, when it's me
own langwidge, and sorrow a bit of another do I know?'
demanded Katy. Then she caught sight of the new
arrival, and stopped short with a blush and a laugh.

'Come in, Mr Worthington,' she said, 'we're at supper,
as you see, and I am acting as waitress.'

'Oh, Uncle Ned, please go away,' pleaded Amy, 'or
Katy will be polite, and not talk Irish any more!'

'Indade, and the less ye say about politeness the
betther, when ye're afther ordering the jantleman out of
the room in that fashion!' said the waitress. Then she
pulled off her cap and untied her apron.

'Now for the Christmas tree,' she said.

It was a very little tree, but it bore some remarkable
fruits, for in addition to the 'tiny toys and candles fit for
Lilliput', various parcels were found to have been hastily
added at the last moment for various people. The
Natchitoches had lately come from the Levant, and delightful Oriental confections now appeared for Amy and
Mrs Ashe; Turkish slippers, all gold embroidery and
towels, with richly decorated ends in silks and tinsel – all
the pretty superfluities which the East holds out to charm

gold from the pockets of her Western visitors. A pretty little dagger in agate and silver fell to Katy's share out of what Lieutenant Worthington called his 'loot'; and beside, a most beautiful specimen of the inlaid work for which Nice is famous – a looking glass with a stand and little doors to close it in – which was a present from Mrs Ashe. It was quite unlike a Christmas Eve at home, but altogether delightful, and as Katy sat next morning on the sand, after the service in the English church, to finish her home letter, and felt the sun warm on her cheek, and the perfumed air blow past as softly as in June, she had to remind herself that Christmas is not necessarily synonymous with snow and winter, but means the great central heat and warmth, the advent of Him who came to lighten the whole earth.

A few days after this pleasant Christmas they left Nice. All of them felt a reluctance to move, and Amy loudly bewailed the necessity.

'If I could stay here till it is time to go home, I shouldn't be homesick at all,' she declared.

'But what a pity it would be not to see Italy!' said her mother. 'Think of Naples and Rome and Venice!'

'I don't want to think about them. It makes me feel as if I was studying a great long geography lesson, and it tires me so to learn it.'

'Amy, dear, you're not well.'

'Yes, I am – quite well; only I don't want to go away from Nice.'

'You only have to learn a little bit at a time of your geography lesson, you know,' suggested Katy, 'and it's a great deal nicer way to study it than out of a book.' But though she spoke cheerfully she was conscious that she shared Amy's reluctance.

'It's all laziness,' she told herself. 'Nice has been so pleasant that it has spoiled me.'

It was a consolation, and made going easier, that they were to drive over the famous Cornice Road as far as San Remo, instead of going to Genoa by rail as most travellers nowadays do. They departed from the Pension Suisse early on an exquisite morning, fair and balmy as June, but with a little zest and sparkle of coolness in the air which made it additionally delightful. The Mediterranean was of the deepest violet blue; a sort of bloom of colour seemed to lie upon it. The sky was like an arch of turquoise; every cape and headland shone jewel-like in the golden sunshine. The carriage, as it followed the windings of the road cut shelf-like on the cliffs, seemed poised between earth and heaven; they saw the sea below, the mountain summits above, and a fairy world of verdure between. The journey was like a dream of enchantment and rapidly-changing surprises, and when it ended in a quaint hostelry at San Remo, with palm trees feathering the Bordighera Point, and Corsica, for once seen by day lying in bold, clear outlines against the sunset, Katy had to admit to herself that Nice, much as she loved it, was not the only, not even the most beautiful place in Europe. Already she felt her horizon growing, her convictions changing, and who should say what lay beyond?

The next day brought them to Genoa, to a hotel once the stately palace of an archbishop, where they were lodged, all three together, in an enormous room, so high and broad and long that their three little curtained beds, set behind a screen of carved wood, made no impression on the space. There were not less than four sofas and double that number of armchairs in the room, besides a couple of monumental wardrobes, but, as Katy remarked, several grand pianos could still have been moved in without anybody feeling crowded. On one side of them lay the port of Genoa, filled with crafts from all parts of the world, and flying the flags of a dozen different nations. From the other they caught glimpses of the magnificent old city, rising in tier over tier of churches and palaces and gardens; while nearer still were narrow streets, which glittered with gold filigree and the shops of jewel workers. And while they went in and out, and gazed and wondered, Lilly Page, at the Pension Suisse, was saying:

'I am so glad that Katy and Mrs Ashe are gone! Nothing has been so pleasant since they came. Lieutenant Worthington is dreadfully stiff and stupid, and seems quite different from what he used to be. But now that we have got rid of them it will all come right again.'

'I really don't think that Katy was to blame,' said Mrs Page. 'She never seemed to me to be making any effort to attract him.'

'Oh, Katy is sly!' responded Lilly vindictively. 'She never *seems* to do anything, but somehow she always gets her own way. I suppose she thought I didn't see her keeping him down there on the beach the other day when he was coming in to call on us, but I did. It was just out of spite, and because she wanted to vex me; I know it was.'

'Well, dear, she's gone now, and you won't be worried with her again,' said her mother soothingly. 'Don't pout so, Lilly, and wrinkle up your forehead. It's very unbecoming.'

'Yes, she's gone,' snapped Lilly, 'and as she's bound for the east, and we for the west, we are not likely to meet again, for which I am devoutly thankful.'

CHAPTER
8

ON THE TRACK OF ULYSSES

'We are going to follow the track of Ulysses,' said Katy, with her eyes fixed on the little travelling map in her guide book. 'Do you realize that, Polly dear? He and his companions sailed these very seas before us, and we shall see the sights they saw – Circe's Cape and the Isles of the Sirens, and Polyphemus himself, perhaps – who knows?'

The *Marco Polo* had just cast off her moorings, and was slowly steaming out of the crowded port of Genoa into the heart of a still rosy sunset. The water was perfectly smooth; no motion could be felt but the engine's throb. The trembling foam of the long wake showed glancing points of phosphorescence here and there, while low on the eastern sky a great silver planet burned like a signal-lamp.

'Polyphemus was a horrible giant. I read about him once, and I don't want to see him,' observed Amy, from her safe protected perch in her mother's lap.

'He may not be so bad now as he was in those old times. Some missionary may have come across him and converted him. If he were good, you wouldn't mind his being big, would you?' suggested Katy.

'N-o,' replied Amy doubtfully, 'but it would take a great lot of missionaries to make *him* good, I should think. One all alone would be afraid to speak to him. We shan't really see him, shall we?'

'I don't believe we shall, and if we stuff cotton in our ears, and look the other way, we need not hear the sirens sing,' said Katy, who was in the highest spirits. 'And oh, Polly dear, there is one delightful thing I forgot to tell you about! The captain says he will stay in Leghorn all day tomorrow taking on freight, and we shall have plenty of time to run up to Pisa and see the cathedral and the Leaning Tower and everything else. Now, that is something Ulysses didn't do! I am so glad I didn't die of measles when I was little, as Rose Red used to say!' She gave her book a toss into the air as she spoke, and caught it again as it fell, very much as the Katy Carr of twelve years ago might have done.

'What a child you are!' said Mrs Ashe approvingly, 'you never seem out of sorts or tired of things.'

'Out of sorts! I should think not! And pray why should I be, Polly dear?'

Katy had taken to calling her friend 'Polly dear' of late – a trick picked up half unconsciously from Lieutenant Ned. Mrs Ashe liked it; it was sisterly and intimate, she said, and made her feel nearer Katy's age.

'Does the tower really lean?' questioned Amy – 'far over, I mean, so that we can see it?'

'We shall know tomorrow,' replied Katy. 'If it doesn't, I shall lose all my confidence in human nature.'

Katy's confidence in human nature was not doomed to be impaired. There stood the famous tower, when they reached the Place del Duomo in Pisa, next morning, looking all aslant, exactly as it does in the pictures and the alabaster models, and seeming as if in another moment it must topple over, from its own weight, upon their heads. Mrs Ashe declared that it was so unnatural that it made her flesh creep, and when she was coaxed up the winding staircase to the top, she turned so giddy that they were all thankful to get her safely down to firm ground again. She turned her back upon the tower, as they crossed the grassy space to the majestic old Cathedral, saying that if she thought about it any more, she should become a disbeliever in the attraction of gravitation, which she had always been told all respectable people *must* believe in.

The guide showed them the lamp, swinging by a long, slender chain, before which Galileo is said to have sat and pondered while he worked out his theory of the pendulum. This lamp seemed a sort of own cousin to the attraction of gravitation, and they gazed upon it with respect. Then they went to the Baptistery to see Niccolo Pisano's magnificent pulpit of creamy marble, a mass of sculpture supported on the backs of lions, and the equally lovely font, and to admire the extraordinary sound which their guide evoked from a mysterious echo, with which he seemed to be on intimate terms, for he made it say whatever he would, and almost 'answer back'.

It was in coming out of the Baptistery that they met with an adventure which Amy could never quite forget. Pisa is the mendicant city of Italy, and her streets are infested with a band of religious beggars who call themselves the Brethren of the Order of Mercy. They wear loose black gowns, sandals laced over their bare feet, and black cambric masks with holes, through which their eyes glare awfully, and they carry tin cups for the reception of offerings, which they thrust into the faces of all strangers visiting the city, whom they look upon as their lawful prey.

As our party emerged from the Baptistery, two of these Brethren espied them, and like great human bats came swooping down upon them with long strides, their black garments flying in the wind, their eyes rolling strangely behind their masks, and brandishing their alms cups, which had 'Pour les Pauvres' lettered upon them, and gave forth a clapping sound like a watchman's rattle. There was something terrible in their appearance and the rushing speed of their movements. Amy screamed and ran behind her mother, who visibly shrank. Katy stood her ground; but the bat-winged fiends in Doré's illustrations to Dante occurred to her, and her fingers trembled as she dropped some money in their cups.

Even mendicant friars are human. Katy ceased to tremble as she observed that one of them, as he retreated, walked backward for some distance in order to gaze longer at Mrs Ashe, whose cheeks were flushed bright pink, and who was looking particularly handsome. She began to laugh instead, and Mrs Ashe laughed too, but Amy could not get over the impression of having been attacked by demons, and often afterwards she shuddered when she thought of those awful black *things* that flew at her and she had hidden behind mamma. The ghastly pictures of the Triumph of Death, which were presently exhibited to them on the walls of the Campo Santo, did not reassure her, and it was with quite a pale, scared little face that she walked toward the hotel where they were to lunch, and she held fast to Katy's hand.

Their way led them through a narrow street inhabited

by the poorer classes – a dusty street with high shabby
buildings on either side and wide doorways giving
glimpses of interior courtyards, where empty hogsheads
and barrels and rusty cauldrons lay, and great wooden
trays of macaroni were spread out in the sun to dry. Some
of the macaroni was grey, some white, some yellow;
none of it looked at all desirable to eat, as it lay exposed to
the dust, with long lines of ill-washed clothes flapping
above on wires stretched from one house to another. As
is usual in poor streets, there were swarms of children,
and the appearance of little Amy with her long bright hair
falling over her shoulders, and Mabel clasped in her
arms, created a great sensation. The children in the street
shouted and exclaimed, and other children within the
houses heard the sounds and came trooping out, while
mothers and older sisters peeped from the doorways.
The very air seemed full of eager faces and little brown
and curly heads bobbing up and down with excitement,
and black eyes fixed upon big beautiful Mabel, who with
her thick wig of flaxen hair, her blue velvet dress and
jacket, feathered hat, and little muff, seemed to them like
some strange small marvel from another world. They
could not decide whether she was a living child or a
make-believe one, and they dared not come near enough
to find out, so they clustered at a little distance, pointed
with their fingers, and whispered and giggled, while
Amy, much pleased with the admiration shown for her
darling, lifted Mabel up to view.

At last one droll little girl with a white cap on her round
head seemed to make up her mind, and, darting indoors,
returned with *her* doll – a poor little image of wood, its
only garment a coarse shirt of red cotton. This she held
out for Amy to see. Amy smiled for the first time since her

encounter with the bat-like friars, and Katy, taking Mabel from her, made signs that the two dolls should kiss each other. But though the little Italian screamed with laughter at the idea of a *bacio* between two dolls, she would by no means allow it, and hid her treasure behind her back, blushing and giggling, and saying something very fast which none of them understood, while she waved two fingers at them with a curious gesture.

'I do believe she is afraid Mabel will cast the evil eye on her doll,' said Katy at last, with a sudden understanding as to what this pantomime meant.

'Why, you silly thing,' cried the outraged Amy, 'do you suppose for one moment that my child could hurt your dirty old dolly? You ought to be glad to have her noticed at all by anybody that's clean.'

The sound of the foreign tongue completed the discomfiture of the little Italian. With a shriek she fled, and all the other children after her, pausing at a distance to look back at the alarming creatures who didn't speak the familiar language. Katy, wishing to leave a pleasant impression, made Mabel kiss her waxen fingers toward them. This sent the children off into another fit of laughter and chatter, and they followed our friends for quite a distance as they proceeded on their way to the hotel.

All that night, over a sea as smooth as glass, the *Marco Polo* slipped along the coasts past which the ships of Ulysses sailed in those legendary days which wear so charmed a light to our modern eyes. Katy roused at three in the morning, and, looking from her cabin window, had a glimpse of an island, which her map showed her must be Elba, where that war eagle, Napoleon, was chained for a while. Then she fell asleep again, and when she awoke in full daylight the steamer was off the coast of

Ostia and nearing the mouth of the Tiber. Dreamy mountain shapes rose beyond the faraway Campagna, and
every curve and every indentation of the coast bore a
name which recalled some interesting thing.

About eleven a dim-drawn bubble appeared on the
horizon, which the captain assured them was the dome
of St Peter's, nearly thirty miles distant. This was one of
the 'moments' which Clover had been fond of speculat-
ing about, and Katy, contrasting the real with the imagin-
ary moment, could not help smiling. Neither she nor
Clover had ever supposed that her first glimpse of the
great dome was to be so unimpressive.

On and on they went till the air-hung bubble disappeared, and Amy, grown very tired of scenery with
which she had no associations, and grown-up raptures
which she did not comprehend, squeezed herself into the
end of the long wooden settee on which Katy sat, and
began to beg for another story concerning Violet and
Emma.

'Just a tiny little chapter, you know, Miss Katy, about
what they did on New Year's Day or something. It's so
dull to keep sailing and sailing all day and have nothing
to do, and it's ever so long since you told me anything
about them, really and truly it is!'

Now, Violet and Emma, if the truth is to be told, had
grown to be the bane of Katy's existence. She had rung
the changes on their uneventful adventures, and racked
her brains to invent more and more details, till her
imagination felt like a dry sponge from which every
possible drop of moisture had been squeezed. Amy was
insatiable. Her interest in the tale never flagged, and
when her exhausted friend explained that she really
could not think of another word to say on the subject, she

would turn the tables by asking, 'Then, Miss Katy, mayn't I tell *you* a chapter?' whereupon she would proceed somewhat in this fashion:

'It was the day before Christmas – no, we won't have it the day before Christmas; it shall be three days before Thanksgiving. Violet and Emma got up in the morning, and – well, they didn't do anything in particular that day. They just had their breakfasts and dinners, and played and studied a little, and went to bed early, you know, and the next morning – well, nothing much happened that day, either; they just had their breakfasts and dinners and played.'

Listening to Amy's stories was so much worse than telling them to her that Katy, in self-defence, was driven to recommence her narrations, but she had grown to hate Violet and Emma with a deadly loathing. So when Amy made this appeal on the steamer's deck, a sudden resolution took possession of her, and she decided to put an end to these dreadful children once and for all.

'Yes, Amy,' she said. 'I will tell you one more story about Violet and Emma, but this is positively the last.'

So Amy cuddled close to her friend, and listened with rapt attention as Katy told how, on a certain day just before the New Year, Violet and Emma started by themselves in a little sleigh drawn by a pony, to carry to a poor woman who lived in a lonely house high up on a mountain slope a basket containing a turkey, a mould of cranberry jelly, a bunch of celery, and a mince pie.

'They were so pleased at having all these nice things to take to poor widow Simpson, and in thinking how glad she would be to see them,' proceeded the naughty Katy, 'that they never noticed how black the sky was getting to be, or how the wind howled through the bare boughs of the trees. They had to go slowly, for the road was uphill all the way, and it was hard work for the poor pony. But he was a stout little fellow, and tugged away up the slippery track, and Violet and Emma talked and laughed, and never thought what was going to happen. Just half way up the mountain there was a rocky cliff which overhung the road, and on this cliff grew an enormous hemlock tree. The branches were loaded with snow, which made them much heavier than usual. Just as the sleigh passed slowly underneath the cliff, a violent blast of wind blew up from the ravine, struck the hemlock, and tore it out of the ground, roots and all. It fell directly across the sleigh, and Violet and Emma and the pony and the basket with the turkey and the other things in it were all crushed as flat as pancakes!'

'Well,' said Amy, as Katy stopped, 'go on! What happened then?'

'Nothing happened then,' replied Katy, in a tone of awful solemnity, 'nothing could happen! Violet and Emma were dead, the pony was dead, the things in the basket were broken all to little bits, and a great snowstorm began and covered them up, and no one knew where they were or what had become of them till the snow melted in the spring.'

With a loud shriek Amy jumped up from the bench.

'No! No! No!' she cried, 'they aren't dead! I won't let them be dead!' Then she burst into tears, ran down the stairs, locked herself into her mother's state room, and did not appear again for several hours.

Katy laughed heartily at first over this outburst, but presently she began to repent and to think that she had treated her pet unkindly. She went down and knocked at the state room door, but Amy would not answer. She called her softly through the key hole, and coaxed and pleaded, but it was all in vain. Amy remained invisible till late in the afternoon, and when she finally crept up again to the deck, her eyes were red with crying, and her little face as pale and miserable as if she had been attending the funeral of her dearest friend.

Katy's heart smote her.

'Come here, my darling,' she said, holding out her hand, 'come and sit in my lap and forgive me. Violet and Emma shall not be dead. They shall go on living, since you care so much for them, and I will tell stories about them to the end of the chapter.'

'No,' said Amy, shaking her head mournfully, 'you can't. They're dead, and they won't come to life again ever. It's all over, and I'm so so-o-rry.'

All Katy's apologies and efforts to resuscitate the story were useless. Violet and Emma were dead to Amy's imagination, and she could not make herself believe in them any more.

She was too woebegone to care for the fables of Circe and her swine which Katy told as they rounded the magnificent Cape Circello, and the isles where the sirens used to sing appealed to her in vain. The sun set, the stars came out, and under the beams of their countless lamps, and the beckonings of a slender new moon, the *Marco Polo* sailed into the Bay of Naples, past Vesuvius, whose dusky curl of smoke could be seen outlined against the luminous sky, and brought her passengers to their landing place.

They woke next morning to a summery atmosphere full of yellow sunshine and July warmth. Flower vendors stood on every corner, and pursued each newcomer with their fragrant wares. Katy could not stop exclaiming over the cheapness of the flowers, which were thrust in at the carriage windows as they drove slowly up and down the streets. They were tied into flat nosegays, whose centre was a white camellia, encircled with concentric rows of pink tea-rosebuds, ring after ring, till the whole was the size of an ordinary milk pan, and all to be had for the sum of ten cents! But after they had bought two or three of these enormous bouquets, and had discovered that not a single rose boasted an inch of stem, and that all were pierced with long wires through their very hearts, she ceased to care for them.

'I would rather have one Souvenir or General Jacqueminot, with a long stem and plenty of leaves, than a dozen of these stiff platters of bouquets,' Katy told Mrs Ashe. But when they drove beyond the city gates, and the coachman came to anchor beneath walls overhung with the same roses, and she found that she might stand on the seat and pull down as many branches of the lovely flowers as she desired, and gather wallflowers for herself out of the clefts in the masonry, she was entirely satisfied.

'This is the Italy of my dreams,' she said.

With all its beauty there was an underlying sense of danger about Naples, which interfered with their enjoyment of it. Evil smells came in at the windows, or confronted them as they went about the city. There seemed something deadly in the air. Whispered reports met their ears of cases of fever, which the landlords of the hotels were doing their best to hush up. An American gentleman was said to be lying very ill at one house. A lady had died the week before at another. Mrs Ashe grew nervous.

'We will just take a rapid look at a few of the principal

things,' she told Katy, 'and then get away as fast as we can. Amy is so on my mind that I have no peace of mind. I keep feeling her pulse and imagining that she does not look right, and though I know it is all my fancy, I am impatient to be off. You won't mind, will you, Katy?'

After that everything they did was done in a hurry. Katy felt as if she were being driven about by a cyclone, as they rushed from one sight to another, filling up all the chinks between with shopping, which was irresistible where everything was so pretty and so wonderfully cheap. She herself purchased a tortoise-shell fan and chain for Rose Red, and had her monogram carved upon it; a coral locket for Elsie; some studs for Dorry; and for her father a small, beautiful vase of bronze, copied from one of the Pompeian antiques.

'How charming it is to have money to spend in such a place as this!' she said to herself, with a sigh of satisfaction, as she surveyed these delightful buyings. 'I only wish I could get ten times as many things and take them to ten times as many people. Papa was so wise about it! I can't think how it is that he always knows beforehand exactly how people are going to feel, and what they will want!'

Mrs Ashe also bought a great many things for herself and Amy, and to take home as presents; it was all very pleasant and satisfactory, except for that subtle sense of danger from which they could not escape and which made them glad to go. 'See Naples and die,' says the old adage, and the saying has proved sadly true in the case of many an American traveller.

Beside the talk of fever there was also a good deal of gossip about brigands going about, as is generally the case in Naples and its vicinity. Something was said to have happened to a party on one of the heights above Sorrento, and though nobody knew exactly what the something was, or was willing to vouch for the story, Mrs Ashe and Katy felt a good deal of trepidation as they entered the carriage which was to take them to the neighbourhood where the mysterious 'something' had occurred.

The drive between Castellamare and Sorrento is in reality as safe as that between Boston and Brookline; but as our party did not know this fact till afterward, it did them no good. It is also one of the most beautiful drives in the world, following the windings of the exquisite coast mile after mile, in long links of perfectly-made road, carved on the face of sharp cliffs, with groves of oranges and lemons and olive orchards above, and the Bay of Naples beneath, stretching away like a solid sheet of lapis-lazuli, and gemmed with islands of the most picturesque form.

It is a pity that so much beauty should have been wasted on Mrs Ashe and Katy, but they were too frightened to half enjoy it. Their carriage was driven by a shaggy young savage, who looked quite wild enough to be a bandit himself. He cracked his whip loudly as they rolled along, and every now and then gave a long shrill whistle. Mrs Ashe was sure that these were signals to his band, who were lurking somewhere on the olive-hung hillsides. She thought she detected him once or twice making signs to certain questionable-looking characters as they passed, and she fancied that the people they met gazed at them with an air of commiseration, as upon victims who were being carried to execution. Her fears affected Katy, so, though they talked and laughed, and made jokes to amuse Amy, who must not be scared or led to suppose that anything was amiss, and to the outward view seemed a very merry party, they were privately quaking in their shoes all the way, and enjoying a deal of highly superfluous misery. And after all they reached Sorrento in perfect safety, and the driver, who looked so dangerous, turned out to be a respectable young man enough, with a wife and family to support, who considered a plateful of macaroni and a glass of sour red wine as the height of luxury, and was grateful for a small gratuity of thirty cents or so, which would enable him to purchase these dainties. Mrs Ashe had a very bad headache next day, to pay for her fright, but she and Katy agreed that they had been very foolish, and resolved to pay no more attention to unaccredited rumours or allow them to spoil their enjoyment, which was a sensible resolution to make.

Their hotel was perched directly over the sea. From the balcony of their sitting room they looked down a sheer cliff some sixty feet high, into the water; their bedrooms opened on a garden of roses, with an orange grove beyond. Not far from them was the great gorge which cuts the little town of Sorrento almost in two, and whose seaward end makes the harbour of the place. Katy was never tired of peering down into this strange and beautiful cleft, whose sides, two hundred feet in depth, are hung with vines and trailing growths of all sorts, and seem all a-tremble with the fairy fronds of maiden-hair ferns growing out of every chink and crevice. She and Amy took walks along the coast toward Massa, to look at the lovely island shapes in the bay, and admire the great clumps of cactus and Spanish bayonet which grew by the roadside, and they always came back loaded with orange flowers, which could be picked as freely as apple blossoms from New England orchards in the spring. The oranges themselves at that time of the year were very sour, but to Katy and her friends they might have been the sweetest in the world.

They made two different excursions to Pompeii, which is within easy distance of Sorrento. They scrambled on donkeys over the hills, and had glimpses of the far-away Calabrian shore, of the natural arch, and the temples of Paestum shining in the sun many miles distant. On Katy's birthday, which fell towards the end of January, Mrs Ashe let her have her choice of a treat, and she elected to go to the island of Capri, which none of them had seen. It turned out a perfect day, with sea and wind exactly right for the sail, and to allow of getting into the famous 'Blue Grotto', which can only be entered under particular conditions of tide and weather. They climbed the great cliff rise at the island's end, and saw the ruins of the villa built by the wicked emperor Tiberius, and the awful place known as his 'Leap', down which, it is said, he made his victims throw themselves; and they lunched at a hotel which bore his name, and just at sunset pushed off again for the row home over the charmed sea. This return voyage was almost the pleasantest thing of all the day. The water was smooth, the moon at its full. It was larger and more brilliant than American moons are, and seemed to possess an actual warmth and colour. The boatmen timed their oar strokes to the cadence of Neapolitan *barcaroles* and folk songs, full of rhythmic movement, which seemed caught from the pulsing tides. And when at last the bow grated on the sands of the Sorrento landing place, Katy drew a long, regretful breath, and declared that this was her best birthday gift of all, better than Amy's flowers, or the pretty tortoise-shell locket that Mrs Ashe had given her, better even than the letter from home, which, timed by happy accident, had arrived by the morning's post to make a bright opening for the day.

But all pleasant things must come to an end.

'Katy,' said Mrs Ashe, one afternoon in early February, 'I heard some ladies talking just now in the *salon*, and they said that Rome is filling up very fast. The carnival begins in less than two weeks. If we don't make haste we shall not be able to get any rooms.'

'Oh dear!' said Katy, 'it is very trying not to be able to be in two places at once. I want to see Rome dreadfully, and yet I cannot bear to leave Sorrento. We have been very happy here, haven't we?'

So they took up their wandering again, and departed for Rome, like the apostle, 'not knowing what should befall them there'.

CHAPTER
9

A ROMAN HOLIDAY

'Oh dear!' said Mrs Ashe, as she folded her letters and laid them aside, 'I wish those Pages would go away from Nice, or else that the frigates were not there.'

'Why! What's the matter?' asked Katy, looking up from the many-leaved journal from Clover over which she was poring.

'Nothing is the matter except that those everlasting people haven't gone to Spain yet, as they said they would, and Ned seems to keep on seeing them,' replied Mrs Ashe petulantly.

'But, dear Polly, what difference does it make? And they never did promise you to go at any particular time, did they?'

'N-o, they didn't; but I wish they would, all the same. Not that Ned is such a goose as really to care anything for that foolish Lilly!' Then she gave a little laugh at her own inconsistency, and added: 'But I oughtn't to abuse her when she is your cousin.'

'Don't mention it,' said Katy cheerfully. 'But, really, I don't see why poor Lilly need worry you so, Polly dear.'

The room in which this conversation took place was on the very topmost floor of the Hotel del Mondo in Rome. It was large and many-windowed, and though there was a little bed in one corner half hidden behind a calico screen, with a bureau and washing-stand, and a sort of stout mahogany hat tree on which Katy's dresses and jackets were hanging, the remaining space, with a sofa and easy chairs grouped round a fire, and a round table furnished with books and a lamp, was ample enough to make a good substitute for the private sitting room which Mrs Ashe had not been able to procure on account of the near approach of the carnival and the consequent crowding of strangers to Rome. In fact, she was assured that under the circumstances she was lucky in finding rooms as good as these, and she made the most of the assurance as a consolation for the somewhat unsatisfactory food and service at the hotel, and the four long flights of stairs which must be passed every time they needed to reach the dining room or the street door.

The party had been in Rome only four days, but already they had seen a host of interesting things. They had stood in the strange sunken space with its marble floor and broken columns, which is all that is left of the great Roman Forum. They had visited the Coliseum, at that period still overhung with ivy garlands and trailing greeneries, and not, as now, scraped clean and bare and 'tidied' out of much of its picturesqueness. They had seen the Baths of Caracalla and the Temple of Janus and St Peter's and the Vatican marbles, and had driven out on the Campagna and to the Pamphili-Doria Villa to gather purple and red anemones, and to the English cemetery to see the grave of Keats. They had also peeped into certain shops, and attended a reception at the American minister's – in short, like most unwarned travellers, they had done about twice as much as prudence and experience would have permitted, had those worthies been consulted.

All the romance of Katy's nature responded to the fascination of the ancient city – the capital of the world, as it may truly be called. The shortest drive or walk brought them face to face with innumerable and unexpected delights. Now it was a wonderful fountain, with plunging horses and colossal nymphs and Tritons, holding cups and horns from which showers of white foam rose high in air to fall like rushing rain into an immense marble basin. Now it was an arched doorway with traceries as fine as lace – sole remaining fragment of a heathen temple, flung and stranded as it were by the wave of time on the squalid shore of the present. Now it was a shrine at the meeting of three streets, where a dim lamp burned beneath the effigy of the Madonna, with always a fresh rose beside it in a vase, and at its foot a peasant woman kneeling in red bodice and blue petticoat, with a lace-trimmed towel folded over her hair. Or again, it would be a sunlit terrace lifted high on a hillside, and crowded with carriages full of beautifully-dressed people, while below all Rome seemed spread out like a panorama, dim, mighty, majestic, and bounded by the blue wavy line of the Campagna and the Alban hills. Or perhaps it might be a wonderful double flight of steps with massive balustrades and pillars with urns, on which sat a crowd of figures in strange costumes and attitudes, who all looked as though they had stepped out of pictures, but who were in reality models waiting for artists to come by and engage them. No matter what it was – a bit of oddly-tinted masonry with a tuft of brown and orange wallflowers hanging upon it, or a vegetable stall where endive and chicory and curly lettuces were arranged in wreaths with tiny orange gourds and scarlet peppers for points of colour – it was all Rome, and, by virtue of that word, different from any other place – more suggestive, more interesting, ten times more mysterious than any other could possibly be, so Katy thought.

This fact consoled her for everything and anything – for the fleas, the dirt, for the queer things they had to eat and the still queerer odours they were forced to smell! Nothing seemed of any particular consequence except the deep sense of enjoyment, and the newly-discovered world of thought and sensation of which she had become suddenly conscious.

The only drawback to her happiness, as the days went on, was that little Amy did not seem quite well. She had taken a cold on the journey from Naples, and though it did not seem serious, that, or something, made her look pale and thin. Her mother said she was growing fast, but the explanation did not quite account for the wistful look in the child's eyes and the tired feeling of which she continually complained. Mrs Ashe, with vague uneasiness, began to talk of cutting short their Roman stay and getting Amy off to the more bracing air of Florence. But meanwhile there was the carnival close at hand, which they must by no means miss, and the feeling that their opportunity might be a brief one made her and Katy all the more anxious to make the very most of their time. So they filled the days full with sights to see and things to do, and came and went, sometimes taking Amy with them, but more often leaving her at the hotel under the care of a kind German chambermaid, who spoke pretty good English and to whom Amy had taken a fancy.

'The marble things are so cold, and the old broken things make me so sorry,' she explained, 'and I hate beggars because they are dirty, and the stairs make my back ache; and I'd a great deal rather stay with Maria and go up on the roof, if you don't mind, Mamma.'

This roof, which Amy had chosen as a play-place, covered the whole of the great hotel, and had been turned into a sort of upper-air garden by the simple process of gravelling it all over, placing trellises of ivy here and there, and setting tubs of oranges and oleanders and boxes of gay geraniums and stock-gillyflowers on the balustrades. A tame fawn was tethered there. Amy adopted him as a playmate, and what with his company and that of the flowers, the times when her mother and Katy were absent from her passed not unhappily.

Katy always repaired to the roof as soon as they came in from their long mornings and afternoons of sight-seeing. Years afterward, she would remember with contrition how pathetically glad Amy always was to see her. She would put her little head on Katy's breast and hold her tight for many minutes without saying a word. When she did speak it was always about the house and the garden that she talked. She never asked any questions as to where Katy had been, or what she had done; it seemed to tire her to think about it.

'I should be very lonely sometimes if it were not for my dear little fawn,' she told Katy once. 'He is so sweet that I don't miss you and mamma very much while I have him to play with. I call him Florio – don't you think that is a pretty name? I like to stay with him a great deal better than to go about with you to those nasty-smelling old churches, with fleas hopping all over them!'

So Amy was left in peace with her fawn, and the others made haste to see all they could before the time came to go to Florence.

Katy realized one of the 'moments' for which she had come to Europe when she stepped for the first time on the balcony, overhanging the Corso, which Mrs Ashe had hired in company with some acquaintances made at the hotel, and looked down at the ebb and surge of the just-begun carnival. The narrow street seemed humming with people of all sorts and conditions. Some were masked, some were not. There were ladies and gentlemen in fashionable clothes, peasants in the gayest costumes, surprised-looking tourists in tall hats and linen dusters, harlequins, clowns, devils, nuns, dominoes of every colour – red, white, blue, black; above, the balconies bloomed like a rose garden with pretty faces framed in lace veils or picturesque hats. Flowers were everywhere wreathed along the house fronts, tied to the horses' ears, in ladies' hands and gentlemen's button holes, while vendors went up and down the street bearing great trays of violets and carnations and camellias for sale. The air was full of cries and laughter, and the shrill calls of merchants advertising their wares – candy, fruit, birds, lanterns, and *confetti*, the latter being merely lumps of lime, large or small, with a pea or a bean embedded in each lump to give it weight. Boxes full of this unpleasant confection were suspended in front of each balcony, with tin scoops to use in ladling it out and flinging it about. Everybody wore or carried a wire mask as protection against this white, incessant shower, and before long the air became full of a fine dust, which hung above the Corso like a mist, and filled the eyes and noses and clothes of all present with irritating particles.

Pasquino's Car was passing underneath just as Katy and Mrs Ashe arrived – a gorgeous affair, hung with silken draperies, and bearing as symbol an enormous egg in which the carnival was supposed to be in act of incubation. A huge wagon followed in its wake, on which was a house some sixteen feet square, whose sole occupant was a gentleman attended by five servants, who kept him supplied with *confetti*, which he showered liberally on the heads of the crowd. Then came a car in the shape of a steamboat, with a smoke pipe and sails, over which flew the Union Jack, and which was manned with a party wearing the dress of British tars. The next wagon bore a company of jolly maskers equipped with many-coloured instruments, which they banged and rattled as they went along. Following this was a troupe of beautiful circus horses, cream coloured with scarlet trappings, or sorrel with blue, ridden by ladies in pale-green velvet laced with silver, or blue velvet and gold. Another car bore a bird cage which was an exact imitation of St Peter's, within which perched a lonely old parrot. This device evidently had a political significance, for it was alternately hissed and applauded as it went along. The whole scene was like a brilliant, rapidly-shifting dream, and Katy, as she stood with lips apart and eyes wide open with wonderment and pleasure, forgot whether she existed or not – forgot everything except what was passing before her gaze.

She was roused by a stinging shower of lime dust. An Englishman on the next balcony had taken courteous advantage of her preoccupation, and had flung a scoopful of *confetti* in her undefended face! It is generally Anglo-Saxons of the less refined class, English or Americans, who do these things at carnival times. The national love of a rough joke comes to the surface, encouraged by the licence of the moment, and all the grace and prettiness of the festival vanish. Katy laughed and dusted herself as well as she could, and took refuge behind her mask, while a nimble American boy of the party changed places with her, and thenceforward made that particular Englishman his special target, plying such a lively and adroit shovel as to make Katy's assailant rue the hour when he evoked this national reprisal. His powdered head and rather clumsy efforts to retaliate excited shouts of laughter from the adjoining balconies. The young American, fresh from tennis and college athletics, darted about and dodged with an agility impossible to his heavily-built foe, and each effective shot and parry on his side was greeted with little cries of applause and the clapping of hands on the part of those who were watching the contest.

Exactly opposite them was a balcony hung with white silk, in which sat a lady who seemed to be of some distinction, for every now and then an officer in brilliant uniform, or some official covered with orders and stars, would be shown in by her servants, bow before her with the utmost deference, and after a little conversation retire, kissing her gloved hand as he went. The lady was a beautiful person, with lustrous black eyes and dark hair, over which a lace mantilla was fastened with diamond stars. She wore pale blue with white flowers, and altogether, as Katy afterwards wrote to Clover, reminded her exactly of one of those beautiful princesses whom they used to act plays about in their childhood and quarrel over, because every one of them wanted to be the princess and nobody else.

'I wonder who she is?' said Mrs Ashe in a low tone. 'She might be almost anybody from her looks. She keeps glancing across to us, Katy. Do you know, I think she has taken a fancy to you.'

Perhaps the lady had, for just then she turned her head and said a word to one of her footmen, who immediately placed something in her hand. It was a little shining bonbonnière, and, rising, she threw it straight at Katy. Alas! It struck the edge of the balcony and fell into the street below, where it was picked up by a ragged little peasant girl in a red jacket, who raised a pair of astonished eyes to the heavens, as if sure that the gift must have fallen straight from there. Katy bent forward to watch its fate, and went through a little pantomime of regret and despair for the benefit of the opposite lady, who only laughed, and, taking another from her servant, flung with better aim, so that it fell exactly at Katy's feet. This was a gilded box in the shape of a mandolin, with sugar plums tucked cunningly away inside. Katy kissed both her hands in acknowledgment for the pretty toy, and tossed back a bunch of roses which she happened to be wearing in her dress. After that it seemed the chief amusement of the fair unknown to throw bonbons at Katy. Some went straight and some did not, but before the afternoon ended, Katy had quite a lapful of confections and trifles – roses, sugared almonds, a satin casket, a silvered box in the shape of a horseshoe, a tiny cage with orange blossoms for birds on the perches, a minute gondola with a *marron glacé* by way of passenger, and, prettiest of all, a little ivory harp strung with enamelled violets instead of wires. For all these favours she had nothing better to offer in return than a few long-tailed bonbons with gay streamers of ribbon. These the lady opposite caught very cleverly, rarely missing one, and kissing her hand in thanks each time.

'Isn't she exquisite?' demanded Katy, her eyes shining with excitement. 'Did you ever see anyone so lovely in your life, Polly dear? I never did. There, now! She is buying those birds to set them free, I do believe.'

It was indeed so. A vendor of larks had, by the aid of a long staff, thrust a cage full of wretched little prisoners up into the balcony, and 'Katy's lady', as Mrs Ashe called her, was paying for the whole. As they watched she opened the cage door, and with the sweetest look on her face encouraged the birds to fly away. The poor little creatures cowered and hesitated, not knowing at first what use to make of their new liberty, but at last one, the boldest of the company, hopped to the door, and with a glad, exultant chirp flew straight upward. Then the others, taking courage from his example, followed, and all were lost to view in the twinkling of an eye.

'Oh, you angel!' cried Katy, leaning over the edge of the balcony and kissing both hands impulsively, 'I never saw anyone so sweet as you are in my life. Polly dear, I think carnivals are the most perfectly bewitching things in the world. How glad I am that this lasts a week, and that we can come every day! Won't Amy be delighted with these bonbons! I do hope my lady will be here tomorrow.'

How little she dreamed that she was never to enter that balcony again! How little can any of us see what lies before us till it comes so near that we cannot help seeing it, or shut our eyes, or turn away!

The next morning, almost as soon as it was light, Mrs Ashe tapped at Katy's door. She was in her dressing gown, and her eyes looked large and frightened.

'Amy is ill,' she cried. 'She has been hot and feverish all night, and she says that her head aches dreadfully. What shall I do, Katy? We ought to have a doctor at once, and I don't know the name of any doctor here.'

Katy sat up in bed, and for one bewildered moment did

not speak. Her brain felt in a whirl of confusion, but presently it cleared, and she saw what to do.

'I will write a note to Mrs Sands,' she said. Mrs Sands was the wife of the American minister, and one of the few acquaintances they had made since they came to Rome. 'You remember how nice she was the other day, and how we liked her, and she has lived here so long that of course she must know all about the doctors. Don't you think that is the best thing to do?'

'The very best,' said Mrs Ashe, looking relieved. 'I wonder I did not think of it myself, but I am so confused that I can't think. Write the note at once, please, dear Katy. I will ring your bell for you, and then I must hurry back to Amy.'

Katy made haste with the note. The answer came promptly in half an hour, and by ten o'clock the physician recommended appeared. Dr Hilary was a dark little Italian to all appearance, but his mother had been a Scots woman, and he spoke English very well – a great comfort to poor Mrs Ashe, who knew not a word of Italian and not a great deal of French. He felt Amy's pulse for a long time, and tested her temperature, but he gave no positive opinion, only left a prescription, and said that he would call later in the day, and should then be able to judge more clearly what the attack was likely to be.

Katy augured ill from this reserve. There was no talk of going to the carnival that afternoon; no one had any heart for it. Instead, Katy spent the time in trying to recollect all she had ever heard about the care of sick people – what was to be done first and what next – and in searching the shops for a feather pillow, which luxury Amy was imperiously demanding. The pillows of Roman hotels are, as a general thing, stuffed with wool, and very hard.

'I won't have this horrid pillow any longer,' poor Amy was screaming. 'It's got bricks in it. It hurts the back of my neck. Take it away, Mamma, and give me a nice soft American pillow. I won't have this a minute longer. Don't you hear me, Mamma? Take it away!'

So, while Mrs Ashe pacified Amy to the best of her ability, Katy hurried out in quest of the desired pillow. It proved almost an unattainable luxury, but at last, after a long search, she secured an air cushion, a down cushion about twelve inches square, and one old feather pillow which had come from some auction, and had apparently lain for years in the corner of the shop. When this was encased in a fresh cover of Canton flannel, it did very well, and stilled Amy's complaints a little; but all night she grew worse, and when Dr Hilary came next day, he was forced to utter plainly the dreaded words 'Roman fever'. Amy was in for an attack – a light one he hoped it might be – but they had better know the truth and make ready for it.

Mrs Ashe was utterly overwhelmed by this verdict, and for the first bewildered moments did not know which way to turn. Katy, happily, kept a steadier head. She had the advantage of a little preparation of thought, and had decided beforehand what it would be necessary to do 'in case'. Oh, that fateful 'in case'! The doctor and she consulted together, and the result was that Katy sought out the *padrona* of the establishment, and without hinting at the nature of Amy's attack, secured some rooms just vacated, which were at the end of a corridor, and a little removed from the rooms of other people. There was a large room with corner windows, a smaller one opening from it, and another, still smaller, close by, which would serve as a storeroom or might do for the use of a nurse.

These rooms, without much consultation with Mrs Ashe – who seemed stunned, and sat with her eyes fixed on Amy, just answering, 'Certainly, dear, anything you say', when applied to – Katy had arranged according to her own ideas of comfort and hygienic necessity, as learned from Miss Nightingale's excellent little book on nursing. From the larger room she had the carpet, curtains, and nearly all the furniture taken away, the floor scrubbed with hot soap suds, and the bed pulled out from the wall to allow a free circulation of air all around it. The smaller one she made as comfortable as possible for the use of Mrs Ashe, choosing for it the softest sofa and the best mattresses that were obtainable, for she knew that her friend's strength was likely to be severely tried if Amy's illness proved serious. When all was ready, Amy, well wrapped in her coverings, was carried down the entry and laid in the fresh bed with the soft pillows about her, and Katy, as she went to and fro, conveying clothes and books and filling drawers, felt that they were perhaps making arrangements for a long, hard trial of faith and spirits.

By the next day the necessity of a nurse became apparent, and in the afternoon Katy started out in a little hired carriage in search of one. She had a list of names, and went first to the English nurses, but, finding them all engaged, she ordered the coachman to drive to a convent where there was hope that a nursing sister might be procured.

Their route lay across the Corso. So utterly had the carnival with all its gay follies vanished from her mind that she was for a moment astonished at finding herself entangled in a motley crowd, so dense that the coachman was obliged to rein in his horses and stand still for some time.

There were the same masks and dominoes, the same picturesque peasant costumes which had struck her as so gay and pretty only three days before. The same jests and merry laughter filled the air, but somehow it all seemed out of tune. The sense of cold, lonely fear that had taken possession of her killed all capacity for merriment; the apprehension and solicitude of which her heart was full made the gay chattering and squeaking of the crowd sound harsh and unfeeling. The bright colours affronted her dejection; she did not want to see them. She lay back in the carriage, trying to be patient through the detention, and half shut her eyes.

A shower of lime dust aroused her. It came from a party of burly figures in white cotton dominoes, whose carriage had been stopped by the crowd close to her own. She signified by gestures that she had no *confetti* and no protection, that she 'was not playing', in fact, but her appeal made no difference. The maskers kept on shovelling lime all over her hair and person and the carriage, and never tired of the sport till an opportune break in the procession enabled their vehicle to move on.

Katy was shaking their largesse from her dress and parasol as well as she could, when she heard an odd gibbering sound close to her ear, and the laughter of the crowd attracted her attention to the back of the carriage. A masker attired as a scarlet devil had climbed into the hood, and was now perched close behind her. She shook her head at him, but he only shook his in return, and chattered and grimaced, and bent over till his fiery mask almost grazed her shoulder. There was no hope but in good humour, as she speedily realized, and, recollecting that in her shopping bag one or two of the carnival bonbons still remained, she took these out and offered them in the hope of propitiating him. The fiend bit one to ensure that it was made of sugar and not lime, while the crowd laughed more than ever; then, seeming satisfied, he made Katy a little speech in rapid Italian, of which she did not comprehend a word, kissed her hand, jumped down from the carriage, and disappeared into the crowd, to her great relief.

Presently after that the driver spied an opening, of which he took advantage. They were across the Corso now, with the roar and rush of the carnival dying into silence as they drove rapidly on, and Katy, as she finished wiping away the last of the lime dust, wiped some tears from her cheeks as well.

'How hateful it all was!' she said to herself. Then she remembered a sentence read somewhere: 'How heavily roll the wheels of other people's joys when your heart is sorrowful!' and she realized that it is true.

The convent was propitious, and promised to send a sister next morning, with the proviso that every second day she was to come back to sleep and rest. Katy was too thankful for any aid to make objections, and drove home with visions of saintly nuns with pure, pale faces full of peace and resignation, such as she had read of in books, floating before her eyes.

Sister Ambrogia, when she appeared next day, did not exactly realize these imaginations. She was a plump little person, with rosy cheeks, a pair of demure black eyes, and a very obstinate mouth and chin. It soon appeared that natural inclination, combined with the rules of her convent, made her theory of a nurse's duties a very limited one.

If Mrs Ashe wished her to go down to the office with an order, she was told: 'We sisters care for the sick; we are not allowed to converse with porters and hotel people.'

If Katy suggested that on the way home she should leave a prescription at the chemist's, it was: 'We sisters are for nursing only; we do not visit shops.' And when she was asked if she could make beef tea, she replied calmly but decisively: 'We are not cooks.'

In fact, all that Sister Ambrogia seemed able or willing to do, beyond the bathing of Amy's face and brushing her hair, which she accomplished handily, was to sit by the bedside telling her rosary, or plying a little ebony shuttle in the manufacture of a long strip of tatting. Even this amount of usefulness was interfered with by the fact that Amy, who by this time was in a semi-delirious condition, had taken an aversion to her at the first glance, and was not willing to be left with her for a single moment.

'I won't stay here alone with Sister Embroidery,' she would cry, if her mother and Katy went into the next room for a moment's rest or a private consultation. 'I hate Sister Embroidery! Come back, Mamma, come back this moment! She's making faces at me, and chattering just like an old parrot, and I don't understand a word she says. Take Sister Embroidery away, Mamma, I tell you! Don't you hear me? Come back, I say!'

The little voice would be raised to a shrill scream, and Mrs Ashe and Katy, hurrying back, would find Amy sitting up on her pillow with wet, scarlet-flushed cheeks and eyes bright with fever, ready to throw herself out of bed, while, calm as Mabel, whose curly head lay on the pillow beside her little mistress, Sister Ambrogia, unaware of the intricacies of the English language, was placidly telling her beads and muttering prayers to herself. Some of these prayers, I do not doubt, related to Amy's recovery, if not to her conversation, and were well meant, but they were rather irritating, under the circumstances!

CHAPTER
10

CLEAR SHINING AFTER RAIN

When the first shock is over and the inevitable realized and accepted, those who tend a long illness are apt to fall into a routine of life which helps to make the days seem short. The apparatus of nursing is got together. Every day the same things need to be done at the same hours and in the same way. Each little appliance is kept at hand, and, sad and tired as the watchers may be, the very monotony and regularity of their proceedings give a certain stay for their thoughts to rest upon.

But there was little of this monotony to help Mrs Ashe and Katy through with Amy's illness. Small chance was there for regularity or exact system, for something unexpected was always turning up, and needful things were often lacking. The most ordinary comforts of the sick room, or what are considered so in America, were hard to come by, and much of Katy's time was spent in devising substitutes to take their places.

Was ice needed? A pailful of dirty snow would be brought in, full of straws, sticks, and other refuse, which had apparently been scraped from the surface of the street after a frosty night. Not a particle of it could be put into milk or water; all that could be done was to make the pail serve the purpose of a refrigerator, and set bowls and tumblers in it to chill.

Was a feeding cup wanted? It came of a cumbrous and antiquated pattern, which the infant Hercules may have enjoyed, but which the modern Amy abominated and rejected. Such a thing as a glass tube could not be found in all Rome. Bed rests were unknown. Katy searched in vain for an india-rubber hot-water bottle.

But the greatest trial of all was the beef tea. It was Amy's sole food, and almost her only medicine, for Dr Hilary believed in leaving nature pretty much to herself in cases of fever. The kitchen of the hotel sent up, under that name, a mixture of grease and hot water, which could not be given to Amy at all. In vain Katy remonstrated and explained the process. In vain did she go to the kitchen herself to translate a carefully written recipe to the cook, and to slip a shining five-franc piece in his hand, which, it was hoped, would quicken his energies and soften his heart. In vain did she order private supplies of the best of beef from a separate market. The cooks stole the beef and ignored the recipe, and day after day the same bottle of greasy liquid came upstairs, which Amy would not touch, and which would have done her no good had she swallowed it all. At last, driven to desperation, Katy procured a couple of stout bottles, and every morning slowly and carefully cut up two pounds of meat into small pieces, sealed the bottle with her own seal ring, and sent it down to be boiled for a specified time. This proved better, for the thieving cook dared not tamper with her seal; but it was a long and toilsome process, and consumed more time than she well knew how to spare – for there were continual errands to be done which no one could attend to but herself, and the interminable flights of stairs taxed her strength painfully, and seemed to grow longer and harder every day.

At last a Good Samaritan turned up in the shape of an American lady with a house of her own who, hearing of their plight from Mrs Sands, undertook to send each day a supply of strong, perfectly-made beef tea from her own kitchen for Amy's use. It was an inexpressible relief, and the lightening of this one particular care made all the rest seem easier of endurance.

Another great relief came, when, after some delay, Dr Hilary succeeded in getting an English nurse to take the places of the unsatisfactory Sister Ambrogia and her substitute, Sister Agatha, whom Amy, in her half-comprehending condition, persisted in calling 'Sister Nutmeg-Grater'. Mrs Swift was a tall, wiry, angular person, who seemed made of equal parts of iron and whalebone. She was never tired; she could lift anybody, and anything, and for sleep she seemed to have a sort of antipathy, preferring to sit in an easy chair and drop off into little dozes, whenever it was convenient, to going regularly to bed for a night's rest.

Amy took to her from the first, and the new nurse managed her beautifully. No one else could soothe her half so well during the delirious period, when the little shrill voice seemed never to be still, and went on all day and all night in alternate raving or screaming, or, what was saddest of all to hear, low pitiful moans. There was no shutting in these sounds. People moved out of the rooms below and on either side, because they could get no sleep, and until the arrival of Nurse Swift, there was no rest for poor Mrs Ashe, who could not keep away from her darling for a moment while that mournful wailing sounded in her ears.

Somehow the long, dry Englishwoman seemed to have a mesmeric effect on Amy, who was never quite so violent after she arrived. Katy was more thankful for this than can well be told, for her great underlying dread – a dread she dared not whisper plainly even to herself – was that 'Polly dear' might break down before Amy was better, and then what *should* they do?

She took every care that was possible of her friend. She made her eat; she made her lie down. She forced daily doses of quinine and port wine down her throat, and saved her every possible step. But no one, however affectionate and willing, could do much to lift the crushing burden of care, which was changing Mrs Ashe's rosy fairness to wan pallor, and laying such dark shadows under the pretty grey eyes. She had taken small thought of her looks since Amy's illness. All the little touches which had made her toilette becoming, all the crimps and fluffs, had disappeared; yet somehow never had she seemed to Katy half so lovely as now in the plain black gown which she wore all day long, with her hair tucked into a knot behind her ears. Her real beauty of feature and outline seemed only enhanced by the rigid plainness of her attire, and the charm of true expression grew in her face. Never had Katy admired and loved her friend so well as during those days of fatigue and wearing suspense, or realized so strongly the worth of her sweetness of temper, her unselfishness and power of devoting herself to other people.

'Polly bears it wonderfully,' she wrote her father. 'She was all broken down for the first day or two, but now her courage and patience are surprising. When I think how precious Amy is to her, and how lonely her life would be if she were to die, I can hardly keep the tears out of my eyes. But Polly does not cry. She is quiet and brave and almost cheerful all the time, keeping herself busy with what needs to be done; she never complains, and she looks – oh, so pretty! I think I never knew how much she had in her before.'

All this time no word had come from Lieutenant Worthington. His sister had written him as soon as Amy was taken ill, and had twice telegraphed since, but no answer had been received, and this strange silence added to the sense of lonely isolation and distance from home and help which those who encounter illness in a foreign land have to bear.

So, first one week and then another wore themselves away somehow. The fever did not break on the fourteenth day, as had been hoped, and must run for another period, the doctor said, but its force was lessened, and he considered that a favourable sign. Amy was quieter now and did not rave so constantly, but she was very weak. All her pretty hair had been shorn away, which made her little face look tiny and sharp. Mabel's golden wig was sacrificed at the same time. Amy had insisted upon it, and they dared not cross her.

'She has got a fever too, and it's a great deal badder than mine is,' she protested. 'Her cheeks are as hot as fire. She ought to have ice on her head, and how can she when her bang is so thick? Cut it all off, every bit, and then I will let you cut mine.'

'You had better give ze child her way,' said Dr Hilary. 'She's in no state to be fretted with triffles [trifles, the doctor meant], and in ze end it will be well, for ze fever infection might harbour in zat doll's head as well as elsewhere, and I should have to disinfect it, which would be bad for ze skin of her.'

'She isn't a dolly,' cried Amy, overhearing him, 'she's my child, and you shan't call her names.' She hugged Mabel tight in her arms, and glared at Dr Hilary defiantly.

So Katy, with pitiful fingers, slashed away at Mabel's blond wig till her head was as bare as a billiard ball, and Amy, quite content, patted her child while her own locks were being cut, and murmured, 'Perhaps your hair will all come out in little round curls, darling, as Johnnie Carr's did,' then she fell into one of the quietest sleeps she had yet had.

It was the day after this that Katy, coming in from a round of errands, found Mrs Ashe standing erect and pale, with a frightened look in her eyes, and her back against Amy's door, as if defending it from somebody. Confronting her was Madame Frulini, the *padrona* of the hotel. Madame's cheeks were red, and her eyes bright and fierce; she was evidently in a rage about something, and was pouring out a torrent of excited Italian, with now and then a French or English word slipped in by way of punctuation, and all so rapidly that only a trained ear could have followed or grasped her meaning.

'What *is* the matter?' asked Katy, in amazement.

'Oh, Katy, I am so glad you have come!' cried poor Mrs Ashe. 'I can hardly understand a word that this horrible woman says, but I think she wants to turn us out of the hotel, and take Amy to some other place. It would be the death of her – I know it would. I never, never will go, unless the doctor says it is safe. I oughtn't to – I couldn't. She can't make me, can she, Katy?'

'Madame,' said Katy – and there was a flash in her eyes before which the landlady rather shrank – 'what is all this? Why do you come to trouble madame while her child is so ill?'

Then came another torrent of explanation which didn't explain, but Katy gathered enough of the meaning to make out that Mrs Ashe was quite correct in her guess, and that Madame Frulini was requesting, nay, insisting, that they should remove Amy from the hotel at once. There were plenty of apartments to be had now that the carnival was over, she said – her own cousin had rooms close by – it could easily be arranged, and people were going away from the Del Mondo every day because there was fever in the house. Such a thing could not be, it should not be; the landlady's voice rose to a shriek, 'The child must go!'

'You are a cruel woman,' said Katy indignantly, when she had grasped the meaning of the outburst. 'It is wicked, it is cowardly, to come thus and attack a poor lady under your roof who has so much already to bear. It is her only child who is lying in there – her only one, do you understand, madame? – and she is a widow. What you ask might kill the child. I shall not permit you or any of your people to enter that door till the doctor comes, and then I shall tell him how you have behaved, and we shall see what he will say.' As she spoke she turned the key of Amy's door, took it out and put it in her pocket, then faced the *padrona* steadily, looking her straight in the eyes.

'Mademoiselle,' stormed the landlady, 'I give you my word, four people have left this house already because of the noises made by little miss. More will go. I shall lose my winter's profit – all of it – all; it will be said there is fever at the Del Mondo – no one will hereafter come to me. There are lodgings plenty, comfortable – oh, so comfortable! I will not have my season ruined by a sickness.'

Madame Frulini's voice was again rising to a scream.

'Be silent!' said Katy sternly. 'You will frighten the child. I am sorry that you should lose any customers, madame, but the fever is here and we are here, and here we must stay till it is safe to go. The child shall not be moved till the doctor gives permission. Money is not the only thing in the world! Mrs Ashe will pay anything that is fair to make up your losses to you, but you must leave this room now, and not return till Dr Hilary is here.'

Where Katy found French for all these long coherent speeches, she could never afterward imagine. She tried to explain it by saying that excitement inspired her for the moment, but that as soon as the moment was over the inspiration died away and left her as speechless and confused as ever. Clover said it made her think of the miracle of Balaam, and Katy merrily rejoined that it might be so, and that no donkey in any age of the world could possibly have been more grateful than was she for the sudden gift of speech.

'But it is not the money – it is my prestige,' declared the landlady.

'Thank Heaven! Here is the doctor now,' cried Mrs Ashe.

The doctor had, in fact, been standing in the doorway for several moments before they noticed him, and had overheard part of the colloquy with Madame Frulini. With him was someone else, at the sight of whom Mrs Ashe gave a great sob of relief. It was her brother at last.

When Italian meets Italian then comes the tug of expletive. It did not seem to take one second for Dr Hilary to whirl the *padrona* out into the entry, where they could be heard going at each other like two furious cats. Hiss, roll, sputter, recrimination, objurgation! In five minutes Madame Frulini was, metaphorically speaking, on her knees, and the doctor standing over her with drawn sword, making her take back every word she had said and every threat she had uttered.

'Prestige of thy miserable hotel!' he thundered, 'where will that be when I go and tell the English and Americans – all of whom I know, every one! – how thou hast served a countrywoman of theirs in thy house! Dost thou think thy prestige will help thee much when Dr Hilary has fixed a black mark on thy door? I tell thee no; not a stranger shalt thou have next year to eat so much as a plate of macaroni under thy base roof! I will advertise thy behaviour in all the foreign papers – in *Figaro*, in *Galignani*, in the *Swiss Times*, and the English one which is read by all the nobility, and the *Heraldo* of New York, which all Americans peruse –'

'Oh, doctor – pardon me – I regret what I said – I am afflicted –!'

'Ik will post thee in the railway stations,' continued the doctor implacably. 'I will bid my patients to write letters to all their friends, warning them against thy flea-ridden Del Mondo. I will apprise the steamboat companies at Genoa and Naples. Thou shalt see what comes of it – truly, thou shalt see.'

Having thus reduced Madame Frulini to powder, the doctor now condescended to take breath and listen to her appeals for mercy, and presently he brought her in with her mouth full of protestations and apologies, and assurances that the ladies had mistaken her meaning; she had only spoken for the good of all; nothing was further from her intention than that they should be disturbed or offended in any way, and she and all her household were at the service of 'the little sick angel of God'. After which the doctor dismissed her with an air of contemptuous tolerance, and laid his hand on the door of Amy's room. Behold, it was locked!

'Oh, I forgot!' cried Katy, laughing, and she pulled the key out of her pocket.

'You are a hee-roine, mademoiselle,' said Dr Hilary. 'I watched you as you faced that tigress, and your eyes were like a swordsman's as he regards his enemy's rapier.'

'Oh, she was so brave, and such a help!' said Mrs Ashe, kissing her impulsively. 'You can't think how she has stood by me all through, Ned, or what a comfort she has been.'

'Yes, I can,' said Ned Worthington, with a warm, grateful look at Katy. 'I can believe anything good of Miss Carr.'

'But where have *you* been all this time?' said Katy, who felt this flood of compliment to be embarrassing. 'We have so wondered at not hearing from you.'

'I have been off on a ten-days' leave to Corsica for moufflon-shooting,' replied Mr Worthington. 'I only got Polly's telegrams and letters the day before yesterday, and I came away as soon as I could get my leave extended. It was a most unlucky absence. I shall always regret it.'

'Oh, it is all right now that you have come!' his sister said, leaning her head on his arm with a look of relief and rest which was good to see. 'Everything will go better now, I am sure.'

'Katy Carr has behaved like a perfect angel,' she told her brother when they were alone.

'She is a trump of a girl. I came in time for part of that scene with the landlady, and upon my word she was glorious! I didn't suppose she could look so handsome.'

'Have the Pages left Nice yet?' asked his sister, rather irrelevantly.

'No – at least they were there on Thursday, but I think that they were to start to-day.'

Mr Worthington answered carelessly, but his face darkened as he spoke. There had been a little scene in Nice which he could not forget. He was sitting in the English garden with Lilly and her mother when his sister's telegrams were brought to him. He had read them aloud, partly as an explanation for the immediate departure which they made necessary, and which broke up an excursion just arranged with the ladies for the afternoon. It is not pleasant to have plans interfered with, and as neither Mrs Page nor her daughter cared personally for little Amy, it is not strange that disappointment at the interruption of their pleasure should have been the first impulse with them. Still, this did not excuse Lilly's unstudied exclamation of 'Oh, bother!', and though she speedily repented it as an indiscretion, and was properly sympathetic, and 'hoped the poor little thing would soon be better', Amy's uncle could not forget the jarring impression. It completed a process of disenchantment which had long been going on, and as hearts are sometimes caught on the rebound, Mrs Ashe was not so far astray when she built certain little dim sisterly hopes on his evident admiration for Katy's courage and this sudden awakening to a sense of her good looks.

But no space was left for sentiment or match-making while still Amy's fate hung in the balance, and all three of them found plenty to do during the next fortnight. The fever did not turn on the twenty-first day, and another weary week of suspense set in, each day bringing a decrease of the dangerous symptoms, but each day as well marking a lessening in the childish strength which had been so long and severely tested. Amy was quite conscious now, and lay quietly, sleeping a great deal and speaking seldom. There was not much to do but to wait and hope, but the flame of hope burned low at times, as the little life flickered in its socket, and seemed likely to go out like a wind-blown torch.

Now and then Lieutenant Worthington would persuade his sister to go with him for a few minutes' drive or walk in the fresh air, from which she had so long been debarred, and once or twice he prevailed on Katy to do the same, but neither of them could bear to be away long from Amy's bedside.

Intimacy grows fast when people are thus united by a common anxiety, sharing the same hopes and fears day after day, speaking and thinking of the same thing. The gay young officer at Nice, who had counted so little in Katy's world, seemed to have disappeared, and the gentle, considerate, tender-hearted fellow who now filled his place was quite a different person in her eyes. Katy began to count on Ned Worthington as a friend who could be trusted for help and sympathy and comprehension, and appealed to and relied upon in all emergencies. She was quite at ease with him now, and asked him to do this and that, to come and help her, or to absent himself, as freely as if he had been Dorry or Phil.

He, on his part, found this easy intimacy charming. In the reaction of his temporary glamour for the pretty Lilly, Katy's very difference from her was an added attraction. This difference consisted, as much as anything else, in the fact that she was so truly in earnest in what she said and did. Had Lilly been in Katy's place, she would probably have been helpful to Mrs Ashe and kind to Amy so far as she could; but the thought of self would have tinctured all that she did and said, and the need of keeping to what was tasteful and becoming would have influenced her in every emergency, and never have been absent from her mind.

Katy, on the contrary, absorbed in the needs of the moment, gave little heed to how she looked or what anyone was thinking about her. Her habit of neatness made her take time for the one thorough daily dressing – the brushing of hair and freshening of clothes, which were customary with her; but, this tax paid to personal comfort, she gave little further heed to appearances. She wore an old grey gown, day in and day out, which Lilly would not have put on for half an hour without a large bribe, so unbecoming was it; but somehow Lieutenant Worthington grew to like the grey gown as a part of Katy herself. And if by chance he brought a rose in to cheer the dim stillness of the sickroom, and she tucked it into her buttonhole, immediately it was as though she were decked for conquest. Pretty dresses are very pretty on pretty people – they certainly play an important part in this queer little world of ours – but depend upon it, dear girls, no woman ever has established so distinct and clear a claim on the regard of her lover as when he has ceased to notice or analyse what she wears, and just accepts it unquestioningly, whatever it is, as a bit of the dear human life which has grown or is growing to be the best and most delightful thing in the world to him.

The grey gown played its part during the long, anxious night when they all sat watching breathlessly to see which way the tide would turn with dear little Amy. The doctor came at midnight, and went away to come again at dawn. Mrs Swift sat grim and watchful beside the pillow of her charge, rising now and then to feel pulse and skin, or to put a spoonful of something between Amy's lips. The doors and windows stood open to admit the air. In the outer room all was hushed. A dim Roman lamp, fed with olive oil, burned in one corner behind a screen. Mrs Ashe lay on the sofa with her eyes closed, bearing the strain of suspense in absolute silence. Her brother sat beside her, holding in his one of the hot hands whose nervous twitches alone told of the surgings of hope and fear within. Katy was resting in a big chair near by, her wistful eyes fixed on Amy's little figure seen in the dim distance, her ears alert for every sound from the sick-room.

So they watched and waited. Now and then Ned Worthington or Katy would rise softly, steal on tiptoe to the bedside, and come back to whisper to Mrs Ashe that Amy had stirred or that she seemed to be asleep. It was one of the nights which do not come often in a lifetime, and which people never forget. The darkness seems full of meaning; the hush, full of sound. God is beyond, holding the sunrise in his right hand, holding the sun of our earthly hopes as well; will it dawn in sorrow or in joy? We dare not ask; we can only wait.

A faint stir of wind and a little broadening of the light roused Katy from a trance of half-understood thoughts. She crept once more into Amy's room. Mrs Swift laid a warning finger on her lips; Amy was sleeping, she said with a gesture. Katy whispered the news to the still figure on the sofa; then she went noiselessly out of the room. The great hotel was fast asleep; not a sound stirred the profound silence of the dark halls. A longing for fresh air led her to the roof.

There was the dawn just tinging the east. The sky, even thus early, wore the deep, mysterious blue of Italy, a fresh *tramontana* was blowing, and made Katy glad to draw her shawl about her.

Far away in the distance rose the Alban Hills above the dim Campagna, with the more lofty Sabines beyond, and Soracte, clear cut against the sky like a wave frozen in the moment of breaking. Below lay that ancient city, with its strange mingling of the old and the new, of past things embedded in the present; or is it the present thinly veiling the rich and mighty past – who shall say?

Faint rumblings of wheels, and here and there a curl of smoke, showed that Rome was waking up. The light insensibly grew upon the darkness. A pink flush lit up the horizon. Florio stirred in his lair, stretched his dappled limbs, and as the first sun ray glinted on the roof, raised himself, crossed the gravelled tiles with soundless feet, and ran his soft nose into Katy's hand. She fondled him for Amy's sake as she stood bent over the flower boxes, inhaling the scent of the mignonette and gillyflowers, with her eyes fixed on the distance, but her heart was at home with the sleepers there, and a rush of strong desire stirred her. Would this dreary time come to end presently, and should they be set at liberty to go their ways with no heavy sorrow to press them down, to be carefree and happy again in their own land?

A footstep startled her. Ned Worthington was coming over the roof on tiptoe, as if fearful of disturbing somebody. His face looked resolute and excited.

'I wanted to tell you,' he said in a hushed voice, 'that

the doctor is here, and he says Amy has no fever, and with care may be considered out of danger.'

'Thank God!' cried Katy, bursting into tears. The long fatigue, the fears kept in check so resolutely, the sleepless night just passed, had their revenge now, and she cried and cried as if she could never stop, but with all the time such joy and gratitude in her heart! She was conscious that Ned had his arm round her and was holding both her hands tight, but they were so one in the emotion of the moment that it did not seem strange.

'How sweet the sun looks!' she said presently, releasing herself, with a happy smile flashing through her tears. 'It hasn't seemed really bright for ever so long. How silly I was to cry! Where is dear Polly? I must go down to her at once. Oh, what does she say?'

CHAPTER
11

NEXT

Lieutenant Worthington's leave had nearly expired. He must rejoin his ship, but he waited till the last possible moment in order to help his sister through the move to Albano, where it had been decided that Amy should go for a few days of hill air before undertaking the longer journey to Florence.

It was a perfect morning in late March when the pale little invalid was carried in her uncle's strong arms, and placed in the carriage which was to take them to the old town on the mountain slopes which they had seen shining from far away for so many weeks past. Spring had come in her fairest shape to Italy. The Campagna had lost its brown and tawny hues and taken on a tinge of fresh colour. The olive orchards were budding thickly. Almond boughs extended their dazzling shapes across the blue sky. Arums and acanthus and ivy filled every hollow, and roses nodded from over every gate, while a carpet of violets and cyclamen and primroses stretched over the fields and freighted every wandering wind with fragrance.

When once the Campagna with its long line of

aqueducts, arches, and hoary tombs, was left behind, and the carriage slowly began to mount the gradual rises of the hill, Amy revived. With every breath of the fresher air her eyes seemed to brighten and her voice to grow stronger. She held Mabel up to look at the view, and the sound of her laugh, faint and feeble as it was, was like music to her mother's ears.

Amy wore a droll little silk-lined cap on her head, over which a downy growth of pale-brown fuzz was gradually thickening. Already it showed a tendency to form into tiny rings, which to Amy, who had always hankered for curls, was an extreme satisfaction. Strange to say, the same thing exactly had happened to Mabel. Her hair had grown out into soft little round curls also; Uncle Ned and Katy had ransacked Rome for this baby wig, which filled and realized all Amy's hopes for her child. On the same excursion they had bought the materials for the pretty spring suit which Mabel wore, for it had been deemed necessary to sacrifice most of her wardrobe as a concession to possible fever germs. Amy admired the pearl-coloured dress and hat, the fringed jacket and little lace-trimmed parasol so much that she was quite consoled for the loss of the blue velvet costume and ermine muff which had been the pride of her heart ever since they left Paris, and whose destruction they had scarcely dared to confess to her.

So up, up, up they climbed till the gateway of the old town was passed, and the carriage stopped before a quaint building, once the residence of the Bishop of Albano, but now known as the Hôtel de la Poste. Here they alighted, and were shown up a wide and lofty staircase to their rooms, which were on the sunny side of the house, and looked across a walled garden, where roses and lemon trees grew beside old fountains guarded by sculptured lions and heathen divinities with broken noses and a scant supply of fingers and toes, to the Campagna, purple with distance, and stretching miles and miles away to where Rome sat on her seven hills, lifting high the dome of St Peter's into the illuminated air.

Nurse Swift said that Amy must go to bed at once and have a long rest. But Amy nearly wept at the proposal, and declared that she was not a bit tired, and couldn't sleep if she went to bed ever so much. The change of air had done her good already, and she looked more like herself than for many weeks past. They compromised their dispute on a sofa, where Amy, well wrapped up, was laid, and where, in spite of her protestations, she presently fell asleep, leaving the others free to examine and arrange their new quarters.

Such enormous rooms as they were! It was quite a journey to go from one side of them to another. The floors were of stone, with squares of carpet laid down over them, which looked absurdly small for the great spaces they were supposed to cover. The beds and tables were of the usual size, but they seemed almost like doll furniture because the chambers were so big. A quaint old paper, with an enormous pattern of banyan trees and pagodas, covered the walls, and every now and then betrayed, by an oblong of regular cracks, the existence of a hidden door, papered to look exactly like the rest of the wall.

These mysterious doors made Katy nervous, and she never rested till she had opened every one of them and explored the places they led to. One gave access to a queer little bathroom. Another led, through a narrow

dark passage, to a sort of balcony or loggia overhanging
the garden. A third ended in a dusty closet with an artful
chink in it from which you could peep into what had been
the bishop's drawing room, but which was now turned
into the dining room of the hotel. It seemed made for
purposes of observation, and Katy had visions of a long
line of reverend prelates with their ears glued to the
chink, overhearing what was being said about them in
the apartment beyond.

The most surprising of all she did not discover till she
was going to bed on the second night after their arrival,
when she thought she knew all about the mysterious
doors and what they led to. A little unexplained draught
of wind made her candle flicker, and betrayed the existence of still another door, so cunningly hidden in the wall
pattern that she had failed to notice it. She had quite a
creepy feeling as she drew her dressing gown about her,
took a light, and entered the narrow passage into which it
opened. It was not a long passage, and ended presently
in a tiny oratory. There was a little marble altar, with a
kneeling step, and candlesticks and a great crucifix
above. Ends of wax candles still remained in the candlesticks, and bunches of dusty paper flowers filled the
vases which stood on either side of them. A faded silk
cushion lay on the step. Doubtless the bishop had often
knelt there. Katy felt as if she were the first person to
enter the place since he went away. Her common sense
told her that in a hotel bedroom, constantly occupied by
strangers for years past, someone *must* have discovered
the door and found the little oratory before her; but
common sense is sometimes less satisfactory than romance. Katy liked to think that she was the first, and to
'make believe' that no one else knew about it. So she did

so, and invented legends about the place which Amy considered better than any fairy story.

Before he left them Lieutenant Worthington had a talk with his sister in the garden. She rather forced this talk upon him, for various things were in her heart about which she longed for explanation; but he yielded so easily to her wiles that it was evident he was not averse to the idea.

'Come, Polly, don't beat about the bush any longer,' he said at last, amused and a little irritated at her half-hints and little feminine *finesses*. 'I know what you want to ask, and as there's no use making a secret of it, I will take my turn in asking. Have I any chance, do you think?'

'Any chance! – about Katy, do you mean? Oh, Ned, you make me so happy!'

'Yes; about her, of course.'

'I don't see why you should say "of course",' remarked his sister, with the perversity of her sex, 'when it's only five or six weeks ago that I was lying awake at night for fear you were being gobbled up by that Lilly Page.'

'There was a little risk of it,' replied her brother seriously. 'She's awfully pretty and she dances beautifully, and the other fellows were all wild about her, and – well, you know yourself how such things go. I can't see now what it was that I fancied so much about her; I don't suppose I could have told exactly at the time; but I can tell without the smallest trouble what it is in – the other.'

'In Katy? I should think so,' cried Mrs Ashe emphatically. 'The two are no more to be compared than – than – well, bread and sillabub! You can live on one and you can't live on the other.'

'Come, now, Miss Page isn't so bad as that. She is a nice girl enough, and a pretty girl too – prettier than Katy;

I'm not so far gone that I can't see that. But we won't talk about her; she's not in the present question at all. Very likely she'd have had nothing to say to me in any case. I was only one out of a dozen, and she never gave me reason to suppose that she cared more for me than the rest. Let us talk about this friend of yours. Have I any chance at all, do you think, Polly?'

'Ned, you are the dearest boy! I would rather have Katy for a sister than anyone else I know. She's so nice all through – so true and sweet and satisfactory.'

'She is all that and more; she's a woman to tie to for life, to be perfectly sure of always. She would make a splendid wife for any man. I'm not half good enough for her; but the question is – and you haven't answered it yet, Polly – what's my chance?'

'I don't know,' said his sister slowly.

'Then I must ask her myself, and I shall do so today.'

'I don't know,' repeated Mrs Ashe. 'She is a woman, therefore to be won, and I don't think there is anyone ahead of you. That is the best hope I have to offer, Ned. Katy never talks of such things, and though she's so frank, I can't guess whether or not she ever thinks about them. She likes you, however, I am sure of that. But, Ned, it will not be wise to say anything to her yet.'

'Not say anything! Why not?'

'No. Recollect that it is only a little while since she looked upon you as the admirer of another girl, and a girl she doesn't like very much, though they are cousins. You must give her time to get over that impression. Wait awhile; that's my advice, Ned.'

'I'll wait any time if only she will say yes in the end. But it's hard to go away without a word of hope, and it's more like a man to speak out, it seems to me.'

'It's too soon,' persisted his sister. 'You don't want her to think you a fickle fellow, falling in love with a fresh girl every time you go into port, and falling out again when the ship sails. Sailors have a bad reputation for that sort of thing. No woman cares to win a man like that.'

'Great Scott! I should think not! Do you mean to say that is the way my conduct appears to her, Polly?'

'No, I don't mean just that. But wait, dear Ned, I am sure it is better.'

Fortified by this sage counsel, Lieutenant Worthington went away next morning, without saying anything to Katy in words, though perhaps eyes and tones may have been less discreet. He made them promise that someone should send a letter every day about Amy, and as Mrs Ashe frequently devolved the writing of these bulletins upon Katy, and the replies came in the shape of long letters, Katy found herself conducting a pretty regular correspondence without quite intending it. Ned Worthington wrote particularly nice letters. He had the knack, more often found in women than men, of giving a picture with a few graphic touches, and indicating what was droll or what was characteristic with a single happy phrase. His letters grew to be one of Katy's pleasures, and sometimes, as Mrs Ashe watched the colour deepen in her cheeks while she read, her heart would bound hopefully within her. But she was a wise woman in her way, and she wanted Katy for a sister very much, so she never said a word or looked a look to startle or surprise her, but left the thing to work itself out, which is the best course always in love affairs.

Little Amy's improvement at Albano was something remarkable. Mrs Swift watched over her like a lynx. Her vigilance never relaxed. Amy was made to eat and sleep and walk and rest with the regularity of a machine, and this exact system, combined with the good air, worked like a charm. The little one gained hour by hour. They could absolutely see her growing fat, her mother declared. Fevers, when they do not kill, operate sometimes as spring bonfires do in gardens, burning up all the refuse and leaving the soil free for the growth of fairer things, and Amy promised in time to be only the better and stronger for her hard experience.

She had gained so much before the time came to start for Florence that they scarcely dreaded the journey, but it proved worse than their expectations. They had not been able to secure a carriage to themselves, and were obliged to share their compartment with two English ladies, and three Roman Catholic priests, one old, the others young. The older priest seemed to be a person of some consequence, for quite a number of people came to see him off, and knelt for his blessing devoutly as the train moved away. The younger ones Katy guessed to be seminary students under his charge. Her chief amusement through the long dusty journey was in watching the terrible time that one of these young men was having with his hat. It was a large three-cornered black affair, with sharp angles and excessively stiff, and a perpetual struggle seemed to be going on between it and its owner, who was evidently unhappy when it was on his head, and still more unhappy when it was anywhere else. If he perched it on his knees it was sure to slide away from him and fall with a thump on the floor, whereupon he would pick it up, blushing furiously as he did so. Then he would lay it on the seat when the train stopped at a station, and jump out with an air of relief; but he invariably forgot, and sat down upon it when he returned, and sprang up with a look of horror at the loud crackle it made. Then he would tuck it into the baggage rack overhead, from which it would presently descend, generally into the lap of one of the staid English ladies, who would hand it back to him with an air of deep offence, remarking to her companion:

'I never knew anything like it. Fancy! That makes four times that hat has fallen on me. The young man is a fidget! He's the most fidgety creature I ever saw in my life.'

The young *seminariat* did not understand a word she said, but the tone needed no interpreter, and set him to blushing more painfully than ever. Altogether, the hat was never off his mind for a moment. Katy could see that he was thinking about it, even when he was thumbing his breviary and pretending to read.

At last the train, steaming down the valley of the Arno, revealed fair Florence sitting among olive-clad hills, with *Giotti*'s beautiful belltower, and the great, many-coloured, soft-hued cathedral, and the square tower of the old Palace, and the quaint bridges over the river, looking exactly as they do in the photographs; and Katy would have felt delighted, in spite of dust and fatigue, had not Amy looked so worn out and exhausted. They were seriously troubled by her, and for the moment could think of nothing else. Happily the fatigue did no permanent harm, and a day or two of rest made her all right again. By good fortune, a nice little apartment in the modern quarter of the city had been vacated by its winter occupants the very day of their arrival, and Mrs Ashe secured it for a month, with all its conveniences and advantages, including a maid named Maria, who had been servant to the just departed tenants.

Maria was a very tall woman, at least six feet two, and had a splendid contralto voice, which she occasionally exercised while busy over her pots and pans. It was so remarkable to hear these grand arias and recitatives proceeding from a kitchen some eight feet square, that Katy was at great pains to satisfy her curiosity about it. By aid of the dictionary and much persistent questioning, she made out that Maria in her youth had received a partial training for the opera, but it was decided that she was too big and heavy for the stage, and the poor 'giantess', as Amy named her, had been forced to abandon her career, and gradually had sunk to the position of a maid-of-all-work. Katy suspected that heaviness of mind as well as of body must have stood in her way, for Maria, though a good-natured giantess, was by no means quick of intelligence.

'I do think that the manner in which people over here can make homes for themselves at five minutes' notice is perfectly delightful,' cried Katy, at the end of their first day's housekeeping. 'I wish we could do the same in America. How cosy it looks here already!'

It was indeed cosy. Their new domain consisted of a parlour in a corner, furnished in bright yellow brocade, with windows to south and west, a nice little dining room, three bedrooms, with dimity-curtained beds, a square entrance hall, lighted at night by a tall slender brass lamp whose double wicks were fed with olive-oil, and the aforesaid tiny kitchen, behind which was a sleeping cubby-hole, quite too small to be a good fit for the giantess. The rooms were full of conveniences – easy chairs, sofas, plenty of bureaus and dressing-tables, and corner fireplaces like Franklin stoves, in which fires burned on cool days. The fires were made of pine cones, cakes of pressed sawdust exactly like Boston brown bread cut into slices, and a few sticks of wood thriftily adjusted, for fuel is worth its weight in gold in Florence. Katy's was the smallest of the bedrooms, but she liked it best of all for the reason that its one big window opened on to an iron balcony, over which grew a Banksia rose vine with a stem as thick as her wrist. It was covered just now with masses of tiny white blossoms, whose fragrance was inexpressibly delicious and made every breath drawn in their neighbourhood a delight. The sun streamed in on all sides of the little apartment, which filled a narrowing angle at the union of three streets, and from one window and another, glimpses could be caught of the distant heights about the city – San Miniato in one direction, Bello Sguardo in another, and for the third the long olive-hung ascent of Fiesole, crowned by its grey cathedral towers.

It was astonishing how easily everything fell into a pattern in the little establishment. Every morning at six the English baker left two small sweet brown loaves and a dozen rolls at the door. Then followed the dairyman with a supply of tiny leaf-shaped pats of freshly-churned butter, a big flask of milk, and two small bottles of thick cream, with a twist of vine leaf in each by way of a cork. Next came a *contadino* with a flask of red Chianti wine, a film of oil floating on top to keep it sweet. People in Florence must drink wine, whether they like it or not, because the lime-impregnated water is unsafe for use without some admixture.

Dinner came from a *trattoria*, in a tin box, with a pan of coals inside to keep it warm; the box was carried on a man's head. It was furnished at a fixed price per day – a soup, two dishes of meat, two vegetables, and a sweet dish, and the supply was so generous as always to leave something toward next day's luncheon. Salad, fruit, and fresh eggs Maria bought for them in the old market. From the confectioner's came loaves of *pane santo*, a sort of light cake made with arrowroot instead of flour, and sometimes, by way of treat, a square of *pan forte da Siena*, compounded of honey, almonds, and chocolate – a mixture as pernicious as it is delicious, and which might take a medal anywhere for the sure production of nightmares.

Amy soon learned to know the shops from which these delicacies came. She had her favourites, too, among the strolling merchants who sold oranges and those little sweet native figs dried in the sun without sugar, which are among the specialities of Florence. They, in their turn, learned to know her and to watch for the appearance of her little capped head and Mabel's blond wig at the window, lingering about till she came, and advertising their wares with musical modulations, so appealing that Amy was always running to Katy, who acted as housekeeper, to beg her to please buy this or that, 'because it is my old man, and he wants me to so much'.

'But, chicken, we have plenty of figs for today.'

'No matter. Get some more, please do. I'll eat them all.'

And Amy was as good as her word. Her convalescent appetite for one so small was something prodigious.

There was another branch of shopping in which they all took equal delight. The beauty and the cheapness of the Florence flowers are a continual surprise to a stranger. Every morning after breakfast an old man came creaking up the two long flights of stairs which led to Mrs Ashe's apartment, tapped at the door, and, as soon as it opened, inserted a shabby elbow and a large flat basket

full of flowers. Such flowers! Great masses of scarlet and
cream-coloured tulips, and white and gold narcissi,
knots of roses of all shades, carnations, heavy-headed
trails of wistaria, wild hyacinths, violets, deep crimson
and orange ranunculus, *giglios*, or wild irises – the
Florence emblem, so deeply purple as to be almost black –
anemones, spring-beauties, faintly tinted wood-blooms
tied in large loose nosegays, ivy, fruit blossoms – everything that can be thought of that is fair and sweet. These
enticing wares the old man would tip out on the table.
Mrs Ashe and Katy would select what they wanted, and
then the process of bargaining would begin, without
which no sale is complete in Italy. The old man would
name an enormous price, five times as much as he hoped
to get. Katy would offer a very small one, considerably
less than she expected to give. The old man would dance
with dismay, wring his hands, assure them that he
should die of hunger, and all his family with him, if he
took less than the price named; he would then come
down half a franc in his demand. So it would go on for
five minutes, ten, sometimes for a quarter of an hour, the
old man's price gradually descending, and Katy's terms
very slowly going up, a cent or two at a time. Next the
giantess would mingle in the fray. She would bounce out
of her kitchen, berate the flower vendor, snatch up his
flowers, declare that they smelt badly, and fling them
down again, pouring out all the while a voluble tirade of
reproaches and revilings, and looking so enormous in
her excitement that Katy wondered that the old man
dared to answer her at all. Finally, there would be a
sudden lull. The old man would shrug his shoulders,
and, remarking that he and his wife and his aged grand-
mother must go without bread that day since it was the

signora's will, would take the money offered and depart, leaving such a mass of flowers behind him that Katy would begin to think that they had paid an unfair price for them and to feel a little rueful, till she observed that the old man was absolutely dancing downstairs with rapture over the good bargain he had made, and that Maria was black with indignation over the extravagance of her ladies!

'The Americani are a nation of spendthrifts,' she would mutter to herself, as she quickened the charcoal in her droll little range by fanning it with a palm-leaf fan. 'They squander money like water. Well, all the better for us Italians!' she would say with a shrug of her shoulders.

'But, Maria, it was only sixteen cents that we paid, and look at those flowers! There are at least half a bushel of them.'

'Sixteen cents for garbage like that! The signorina would better let me make her bargains for her. *Già! Già!* No Italian lady would have paid more than eleven sous for such useless *roba*. It is evident that the signorina's countrymen eat gold when at home, they think so little of casting it away!'

Altogether, what with the comfort and quiet of this little home, the numberless delightful things that there were to do and to see, and Viessieux's great library, from which they could draw books at will to make the doing and seeing more intelligible, the month at Florence passed only too quickly, and was one of the times to which they afterward looked back with most pleasure. Amy grew steadily stronger, and the freedom from anxiety about her after their long strain of apprehension was restful and healing beyond expression to both mind and body.

Their very last excursion of all, and one of the pleasantest, was to the old amphitheatre at Fiesole, and it was while they sat there in the soft glow of the late afternoon, tying into bunches the violets which they had gathered from under walls whose foundations pre-date Rome itself, that a cheery call sounded from above, and an unexpected surprise descended upon them in the shape of Lieutenant Worthington, who, having secured another fifteen days' furlough, had come to take his sister on to Venice.

'I didn't write you that I had applied for leave,' he explained, 'because there seemed so little chance of my getting off again so soon, but as luck had it, Carruthers, whose turn it was, sprained his ankle and was laid up, and the commodore let us exchange. I made all the capital I could out of Amy's fever, but upon my word, I felt like a humbug when I came upon her and Mrs Swift in the Cascine just now, as I was hunting for you. How she has picked up! I should never have known her for the same child.'

'Yes, she seems perfectly well again, and as strong as before she had the fever, though that dear old Goody Swift is just as careful of her as ever. She would not let us bring her here this afternoon, for fear we should stay out till the dew fell. Ned, it is perfectly delightful that you were able to come. It makes going to Venice seem quite a different thing, doesn't it, Katy?'

'I don't want it to seem quite different, because going to Venice was always one of my dreams,' replied Katy, with a little laugh.

'I hope at least it doesn't make it seem less pleasant,' said Mr Worthington, as his sister stopped to pick a violet.

'No, indeed, I am glad,' said Katy. 'We shall all be seeing it for the first time, too, shall we not? I think you said you had never been there.' She spoke simply and frankly, but she was conscious of an odd shyness.

'I simply couldn't stand it any longer,' Ned Worthington confided to his sister when they were alone. 'My head is so full of her that I can't attend to my work, and it came to me all of a sudden that this might be my last chance. You'll be getting north before long, you know, to Switzerland and so on, where I cannot follow you. So I made a clean breast of it to the commodore, and the good old fellow, who has a soft spot in his heart for a love story, behaved like a brick, and made it all straight for me to come away.'

Mrs Ashe did not join in these commendations of the commodore; her attention was fixed on another part of her brother's discourse.

'Then you won't be able to come to me again? I shan't see you again after this!' she exclaimed. 'Dear me! I never realized that before. What shall I do without you?'

'You will have Miss Carr. She is a host in herself,' suggested Ned Worthington. His sister shook her head.

'Katy is a jewel,' she remarked presently, 'but somehow one wants a man to call upon. I shall feel lost without you, Ned.'

The month's housekeeping wound up that night with a 'thick tea' in honour of Lieutenant Worthington's arrival, which taxed all the resources of the little establishment. Maria was sent out hastily to buy *pan forte da Siena* and *vino d'Asti*, and fresh eggs for an omelette, and chickens' breasts smothered in cream from the restaurant, and artichokes for a salad, and flowers to garnish all. The guest ate and praised and admired; Amy and

Mabel sat on his knee and explained everything to him, and they were all very happy together. Their merriment was so infectious that it extended to the poor giantess, who had been very pensive all day at the prospect of losing her good place, and who now raised her voice in the grand aria from *Orfeo*, and made the kitchen ring with the passionate demand, *'Che faro senza, Eurydice?'* The splendid notes, full of fire and lamentation, rang out across saucepans as effectively as if they had been foot-lights, and Katy, rising softly, opened the kitchen door a little way that they might not lose a sound.

The next day brought them to Venice. It was a 'moment', indeed, as Katy seated herself for the first time in a gondola, and looked from beneath its black hood at the palace walls on the Grand Canal, past which they were gliding. Some were creamy and white and black, some orange-tawny, others of a dull, delicious ruddy colour, half-pink, half-red; but all, in build and orna-ment, were unlike palaces elsewhere. High on the prow before her stood the gondolier, his form defined in dark outline against the sky, as he swayed and bent to his long oar, raising his head now and again to give a wild musical cry, as warning to other approaching gondolas. It was all like a dream. Ned Worthington sat beside her, looking more at the changes in her expressive face than at the palaces. Venice was as new to him as to Katy, but she was also a new feature in his life, and even more interesting than Venice.

They seemed to float on pleasures for the next ten days. Their arrival had been happily timed to coincide with a great popular festival, which for nearly a week kept Venice in a state of continual brilliant gala. All the days were spent on the water, only landing now and then to look at some famous building or picture, or to eat ices in the Piazza with the lovely façade of St Mark's before them. Dining or sleeping seemed a sheer waste of time! The evenings were spent on the water too, for every night, immediately after sunset, a beautiful drifting pageant started from the front of the Doge's Palace to make the tour of the Grand Canal, and our friends always took a part in it. In its centre went a barge hung with embroideries, and filled with orange trees and musicians. This was surrounded by a great convoy of skiffs and gondolas bearing coloured lanterns and streamers and gay awnings, and managed by gondoliers in picturesque uniforms. All these floated and shifted and swept on together with a sort of rhythmic undulation, as if keeping time to the music, while across their path dazzling showers and arches of coloured fire poured from the palace fronts and the hotels. Every movement of the fairy flotilla was repeated in the illuminated water, with every torch tip and scarlet lantern and flake of green or rosy fire. Above it all the bright full moon looked down as if surprised. It was magically beautiful in effect. Katy felt as if her previous sober ideas about life and things had melted away. For the moment the world was turned topsy-turvy. There was nothing hard or real or sordid left in it; it was just a fairy tale, and she was in the middle of it as she had longed to be in her childhood. She was the princess, encircled by delights, as when she and Clover and Elsie played in 'Paradise' – only, this was better. And, dear me! who was this prince who seemed to belong to the story and to grow more important to it every day?

Fairy tales must come to an end. Katy's last chapter closed with a sudden turnover of the leaf, when towards the end of this happy fortnight, Mrs Ashe came into her room with the face of one who has unpleasant news to communicate.

'Katy,' she began, 'should you be *awfully* disappointed, should you consider me a perfect wretch, if I went home now instead of in the autumn?'

Katy was too much astonished to reply.

'I am grown such a coward. I am so knocked up and weakened by what I suffered in Rome, that I find I cannot face the idea of going on to Germany and Switzerland alone, without Ned to take care of me. You are a perfect angel, dear, and I know that you would do all you could to make it easy for me, but I am such a fool that I do not dare. I think my nerves must have given way,' she continued half tearfully, 'but the very idea of shifting for myself for five months longer makes me so miserably homesick that I cannot endure it. I dare say I shall repent afterward, and I tell myself now how silly it is, but it's no use – I shall never know another easy moment till I have Amy safe again in America and under your father's care.

'I find,' she continued, after another little pause, 'that we can go down with Ned to Genoa and take a steamer there which will carry us straight to New York without any stops. I hate to disappoint you dreadfully, Katy, but I have almost decided to do it. Shall you mind very much? Can you ever forgive me?' She was fairly crying now.

Katy had to swallow hard before she could answer, for the sense of disappointment was so sharp, and with all her efforts there was almost a sob in her voice as she said:

'Why, yes, indeed, dear Polly, there is nothing to forgive. You are perfectly right to go home if you feel so.' Then with another swallow she added, 'You have given me the loveliest six months' treat that ever was, and I should be a greedy girl indeed if I found fault because it is cut off a little sooner than we expected.'

'You are so dear and good not to be vexed,' said her friend, embracing her. 'It makes me feel doubly sorry about disappointing you. Indeed I wouldn't if I could help it, but I simply can't. I *must* go home. Perhaps we'll come back some day when Amy is grown up, or safely married to somebody who will take good care of her!'

This distant prospect was but a poor consolation for the immediate disappointment. The more Katy thought about it the sorrier did she feel. It was not only losing the chance – very likely the only one she would ever have – of seeing Switzerland and Germany; it was all sorts of other little things besides. They must go home in a strange ship with a captain they did not know, instead of in the *Spartacus*, as they had planned; they should land in New York, where no one would be waiting for them, and not have the fun of sailing into Boston Bay and seeing Rose on the wharf, where she had promised to be. Furthermore, they must pass the hot summer in Burnet instead of in the cool Alpine valleys, and Polly's house was let till October. She and Amy would have to shift for themselves elsewhere. Perhaps they would not be in Burnet at all. Oh, dear, what a pity it was! What a dreadful pity!

Then, the first shock of surprise and discomfiture over, other ideas asserted themselves, and as she realized that in three weeks more, or four at the longest, she was to see Papa and Clover and all her dear people at home, she began to feel so very glad that she could hardly wait for the time to come. After all there was nothing in Europe quite so good as that.

'No, I'm not sorry,' she told herself. 'I am glad. Poor Polly! It's no wonder she feels nervous after all she has gone through. I hope I wasn't cross to her! And it will be *very* nice to have Lieutenant Worthington to take care of us as far as Genoa.'

The next three days were full of work. There was no more floating in gondolas, except in the way of business. All the shopping which they had put off must be done, and the trunks packed for the voyage. Everyone recollected last errands and commissions; there was continual coming and going and confusion, and Amy, wild with excitement, popping up every other moment in the midst of it all, to demand of everybody if they were not glad that they were going back to America.

Katy had never yet bought her gift for old Mrs Redding. She had waited, thinking continually that she should see something more tempting still in the next place they went to, but now, with the sense that there were to be no more 'next places', she resolved to wait no longer, and with a hundred francs in her pocket, set forth to choose something from among the many tempting things for sale in the Piazza. A bracelet of old Roman coins had caught her fancy one day in a bric-à-brac shop, and she walked straight towards it, only pausing by the way to buy a pale blue iridescent pitcher at Salviate's for Cecy Slack, and see it carefully rolled in seaweed and soft paper.

The price of the bracelet was a little more than she expected, and quite a long process of bargaining was necessary to reduce it to the sum she had to spend. She had just succeeded, and was counting out the money, when Mrs Ashe and her brother appeared, having spied her from the opposite side of the Piazza, where they were choosing last photographs at Naga's. Katy showed her purchase and explained that it was a present, 'for of course I should never walk out in cold blood and buy a bracelet for myself,' she said, with a laugh.

'This is a fascinating little shop,' said Mrs Ashe. 'I wonder what is the price of that queer old chatelaine with the bottles hanging from it.'

The price was high, but Mrs Ashe was now tolerably conversant with shopping Italian, which consists chiefly of a few words repeated many times over, and it lowered rapidly under the influence of her *troppo*'s and *è molto caro*'s, accompanied with telling little shrugs and looks of surprise. In the end she bought it for less than two-thirds of what had been originally asked for it. As she put the parcel in her pocket, her brother said:

'If you have done your shopping now, Polly, can't you come out for a last row?'

'Katy may, but I can't,' replied Mrs Ashe. 'The man promised to bring me gloves at six o'clock, and I must be there to pay for them. Take her down to the Lido, Ned. It's an exquisite evening for the water, and the sunset promises to be delicious. You can take the time, can't you, Katy?'

Katy could.

Mrs Ashe turned to leave them, but suddenly stopped short.

'Katy, look! Isn't that a picture?'

The 'picture' was Amy, who had come to the Piazza with Mrs Swift, to feed the doves of St Mark's, which was one of her favourite amusements. These pretty birds are the pets of all Venice, and so accustomed to being fondled and made much of by strangers that they are perfectly tame. Amy, when her mother caught sight of her, was sitting on the marble pavement, with one on her shoulder, two perched on the edge of her lap, which was full of crumbs, and a flight of others circling round her head. She was looking up and calling them in soft tones. The sunlight caught the little downy curls on her head and made them glitter. The flying doves lit on the pavement, and crowded round her, their pearl and grey and rose-tinted and white feathers, their scarlet feet and gold-ringed eyes, making a shifting confusion of colours, as they hopped and fluttered and cooed about the little maid, unstartled even by her clear laughter. Close by stood Nurse Swift, observant and grimly pleased.

The mother looked on with happy tears in her eyes. 'Oh, Katy, think what she was a few weeks ago, and look at her now! Can I ever be thankful enough?'

She squeezed Katy's hand convulsively and walked away, turning her head now and then for another glance at Amy and the doves, while Ned and Katy silently crossed to the landing and got into a gondola. It was the perfection of a Venice evening, with silver waves lapsing and lulling under a rose and opal sky, and the sense that it was their last row on those enchanted waters made every moment seem doubly precious.

I cannot tell you exactly what it was that Ned Worthington said to Katy during that row, or why it took so long to say it that they did not get in till after the sun was set, and the stars had come out to peep at their bright, glinting faces reflected in the Grand Canal. In fact, no one can tell, for no one overheard, except Giacomo, the brown yellow-jacketed gondolier, and as he did not understand a word of English he could not repeat the conversation. Venetian boatmen, however, know pretty well what it means when a gentleman and lady, both young, find so much to say in low tones to each other under the gondola hood, and are so long about giving the order to return and Giacomo, deeply sympathetic, rowed as softly and made himself as imperceptible as he could – a display of tact which merited the big silver piece with which Lieutenant Worthington 'crossed his palm' on landing.

Mrs Ashe had begun to look for them long before they appeared, but I think she was neither surprised nor sorry that they were so late. Katy kissed her hastily and went away at once – 'to pack', she said – and Ned was equally undemonstrative, but they looked so happy, both of them, that 'Polly dear' was quite satisfied and asked no questions.

Five days later the parting came, when the *Florio* steamer put into the port of Genoa for passengers. It was not an easy goodbye to say. Mrs Ashe and Amy both cried, and Mabel was said to be in deep affliction also. But there were alleviations. The squadron was coming home in the autumn, and the officers would have leave to see their friends, and of course Lieutenant Worthington must come to Burnet – to visit his sister. Five months would soon go, he declared, but, for all the cheerful assurance, his face was rueful enough as he held Katy's hand in a long tight clasp while the little boat waited to take him ashore.

After that it was just the waiting to be got through with till they sighted Sandy Hook and the Neversinks – a waiting varied with peeps at Marseilles and Gibraltar, and the sight of a whale or two and one distant iceberg. The weather was fair all the way, and the ocean smooth. Amy was never weary of lamenting her own stupidity in not having taken Maria Matilda out of confinement before they left Venice.

'That child has hardly been out of the trunk since we

started,' she said. 'She hasn't seen anything except a little bit of Nice. I shall really be ashamed when the other children ask her about it. I think I shall play that she was left at boarding school and didn't come to Europe at all! Don't you think that would be the best way, Mamma?'

'You might play that she was left in the States prison for having done something naughty,' suggested Katy, but Amy scouted this idea.

'She never does naughty things,' she said, 'because she never does anything at all. She's just stupid, poor child! It's not her fault.'

The thirty-six hours between New York and Burnet seemed longer than all the rest of the journey put together, Katy thought. But they ended at last, as the *Lake Queen* swung to her moorings at the familiar wharf, where Dr Carr stood surrounded with all his boys and girls just as they had stood the previous October. Only now there were no clouds on anybody's face, and Johnnie was skipping up and down for joy instead of grief. It was a long moment while the plank was being lowered from the gangway, but the moment it was in place, Katy darted across, first ashore of all the passengers, and was in her father's arms.

Mrs Ashe and Amy spent two or three days with them, while looking up temporary quarters elsewhere, and so long as they stayed all seemed a happy confusion of talking and embracing and explaining, and distributing of gifts. After they went away things fell into their customary train, and a certain flatness became apparent. Everything had happened that could happen. The long-talked-of European journey was over. Here was Katy at home again, months sooner than they expected, yet she looked remarkably cheerful and content! Clover could not understand it: she was likewise puzzled to account for one or two private conversations between Katy and Papa in which she had not been invited to take part, and the occasional arrival of a letter from 'foreign parts' about whose contents nothing was said.

'It seems a dreadful pity that you had to come so soon,' she said one day when they were alone in their bedroom. 'It's delightful to have you, of course, but we had braced ourselves to do without you till October, and there are such a lot of delightful things that you could have been doing and seeing at this moment.'

'Oh, yes, indeed!' replied Katy, but not at all as if she were particularly disappointed.

'Katy Carr, I don't understand you,' persisted Clover. 'Why don't you feel worse about it? Here you have lost five months of the most splendid time you ever had, and you don't seem to mind it a bit! Why, if I were in your place my heart would be perfectly broken. And you needn't have come, either; that's the worst of it. It was just a whim of Polly's. Papa says Amy might have stayed as well as not. Why aren't you sorrier, Katy?'

'Oh, I don't know! Perhaps because I had so much as it was – enough to last all my life, I think, though I *should* like to go again. You can't imagine what beautiful pictures are put away in my memory.'

'I don't see that you had so awfully much,' said the aggravated Clover. 'You were there only a little more than six months – for I don't count the sea – and ever so much of that time was taken up with nursing Amy. You can't have any pleasant pictures of *that*.'

'Yes, I have; some.'

'Well, I should really like to know what. There you were in a dark room, frightened to death and tired to death, with only Mrs Ashe and the old nurse to keep you company. Oh, yes, that brother was there part of the time! I forgot him –'

Clover stopped short in sudden amazement. Katy was standing with her back towards her, smoothing her hair, but her face was reflected in the glass. At Clover's words a sudden deep flush had mounted in Katy's cheeks. Deeper and deeper it burned as she became conscious of Clover's astonished gaze, till even the back of her neck was pink. Then, as if she could not bear it any longer, she put the brush down, turned, and fled out of the room, while Clover, looking after her, exclaimed in a tone of sudden comical dismay:

'What does it mean? Oh, dear me! Is *that* what Katy is going to do next?'